Cut & Drag

Tips & Tricks for Filmmaking Freaks

by
Fabrizio Gammardella
(Video Editor)

ISBN: 979-12-210-2881-2

Illustrations by Veronica Spinoni
Graphic Design and Cover by Fabrizio Gammardella

This book is dedicated to my father,
who ignited the spark
and to Mr Takeshi Kitano,
whose unparalleled genius
still inspires me every day.

TABLE OF CONTENTS

INTRODUCTION

I'll cut to the chase (pun intended of course). The reason I wrote this *handbook* is simple: to share with fellow colleagues, newcomers and film students, a quick overview on fundamental *editing and film-making principles* which I reckon professionals and newcomers can't do without. The very core, easy to go through and stripped to the bone. The kind of info you want to bring with you on set everyday to jog your memory about this or that matter.

***

I've always been a movie freak, obsessed since childhood with Asian cinema, animated series and black and white flicks. I've watched Akira Kurosawa's *Seven Samurai* dozens of times, laughed my head off at Kikuchiyo's jokes and cried my eyes out when he passes away after giving it all on the battlefield. I was only twelve or thirteen years old and I couldn't grasp why that movie was having such a profound impact on my life. Why did I empathise so much with the characters, getting in tune with their emotions, and feeling myself the same pain and distress they were showing on the screen? There was something missing in my viewer's toolbox. I knew nothing about editing, storytelling, structure, character's arc and development. It was only the thrill, the immersive experience of witnessing someone else's life unfold in real time in front of my eyes. Samurai warriors from Japan's Sengoku period (1467-1615) suddenly brought back to the 20th century! The illusion was so vivid and tangible that It didn't matter that it was only a VCR playing a tape on a CRT television set. Right there and then, it felt as if I was with those samurai warriors.

By the time I turned eighteen, even though my passion for cinema still burned inside me, I found myself studying Law at the University of Naples Federico II, trying to earn a degree to open countless doors for a brilliant future in the Legal

Profession. If I'd only known back then how things would turn out for me... I wouldn't have stressed out so much over laws, articles and codes. It was around this time that something clicked into place. I stopped watching films just as films, but started wondering why the film-makers did what they did. Why did the editor cut in a certain place, why did the character act so tough in one scene and so vulnerable in another? Why did the DOP choose to get that slanted camera angle, why the dark cinematography? Internet wasn't a big thing back then (I'm from 1985), so I couldn't just look everything up on my smartphone while on my way to the University. The only reliable way to dive deep into any matter, was still through books and manuals. And here's the turning point in my story – the "big event" – that revealing moment which dramatically affects the central character's life, kicking things out of balance and making the hero reach a crossroads: I stumbled onto a book called *Grammar of the film language,* by Daniel Arijon.

This is a highly technical behemoth of more than 600 pages. A very unique guide to the visual narrative techniques that form the "language" of film-making. I won't lie, it took me many years to go through it. At the beginning it was so frustrating, I couldn't believe that there was so much to learn about filming techniques, camera arrangements and angles, editing patterns, blocking scenes and so on. How the hell could someone keep all that stuff in mind while shooting or planning a movie? It was too much for an average guy to process or handle, I was ready to give up on my passion for cinema and settle for going to the theatres with the boys once in a while, to enjoy the latest movie sensation coming from the US. Why would I want to add something else on top of my the University engagements? That book required a degree in film-making itself to be understood. And being packed with more than 1500 illustrations wasn't actually much help. Each of the illustrations and shooting plans were so complicated that I couldn't get my head around them. How was I supposed to know anything about the 180-Degree rule? Does continuity really matter? Why can't someone just place the camera anywhere they want or where the shot looks cooler?

I finally got to grips with it. I became so obsessed with film-making and ended up spending hours studying those shooting plans and camera arrangements. I began to see the "pattern" the author was talking about and a new reality unfolded right in front of my eyes: the world of the "makers" and that of the "viewers". My thirst spread to the History of cinema as well. George Méliès, Auguste e Louis Lumière, Alice Guy, Max Linder, David W. Griffith, Edwin S. Porter, Sergei Eisenstein, George Albert Smith, Leopoldo Fregoli. Who were these people? Did it really matter to learn about their pioneering work during the first decades since the birth of the cinema? Is their legacy that important after all? I started to wonder if I could emulate them, belonging to that elite group who could actually "make" those wonderful movies I was so fond of. Perhaps I could lead someone else to the path of joy, sorrow or excitement through my new acquired knowledge of the cinema rules and principles. If you're reading this book you know what all the fuss is about. I eventually became a video editor: years of struggle, thousands of miles away from my family, catapulted from a tiny town of 10,000 souls to the beautiful 9 million people of London (not all of them though, I did bump into some jerks along the way). Countless hours studying handbooks, manuals, scraps of papers, absorbing every tiny piece of information which could lead me to my goal of being a skilled professional, someone directors and producers could rely on. What I do know, is that I've been blessed enough to make a living as a video editor for more than the past decade and things ahead look more exciting than ever.

***

So back to this handbook. I'm giving you a quick overview on the core principles of our craft, those which don't age as new filming techniques and technologies come about. You'll notice that I use the word "rules" from time to time throughout the book. This is for ease of understanding, there aren't any rules per se and you should feel free to innovate and bend and break any "rules" you read about here. Once you've mastered them, of course. To quote Polonius: *"Though this be madness, yet there is method in't"*. And there is indeed method and discipline in what editors in particular do every day in the isolation of the editing room (and outside of it too). This book amounts to more than 5 years of painstaking research, a crazy effort to "update" Arijon's book, Photoshopping new shooting plans – based on actual movies and TV series and illustrated by the talented Veronica Spinoni – which help clarify concepts that at a first glance seem too complicated to the reader, especially when approaching some highly technical principles of our craft.

This handbook is by no means a complete guide to the ever-changing and evolving world of editing and film-making. Such an ambitious goal would be beyond the scope of what can be achieved through the mere study of books. Get your hands dirty, put the theory to the test and into practice. No editing manual can teach you when a cut is "right". You need to scrub through hours and hours of footage for many, many years before being able to "feel" that the cut is perfect and the pace and flow of your edit impeccable. Feel free to jump from one chapter to another, if you need to, or skip an entire section or just check the most common camera arrangements used to cover a three-player dialogue. Bring this manual with you on set and leaf through the pages to jog your memory about anything which might come in handy during a shooting or in the darkness of the editing room. No matter how you make the most of the book's content, please never forget that no film-making concept is too complicated to be grasped, no editing principle is set in stone. This book won't get you out of trouble while cutting a scene that doesn't shape up as expected, if its pace lacks the fluidity required to deliver strong emotions to the audience. That is stuff that simply cannot be taught. You will learn this yourself, on the job. From time to time you may struggle to grasp some of the terminology used throughout the chapters. Take to the Internet.

After all: *"Curiosity is the mother of all knowledge"*.

PART
ONE

1

EDITING & FILM-MAKING *ARE* STORYTELLING

1.1 ● Catalyst

1.2 ● Big event

1.3 ● Pinch

1.4 ● Crisis

1.5 ● Showdown

1.6 ● Realization

Screenwriters, film-makers and editors strive every day to find new, creative ways to unfold and disclose the narrative of a story: subtle, little moments that make audiences aware that the story is moving forward and something is about to happen. This magic process that triggers our emotions and keeps us engaged when watching a movie, is called *storytelling.* A well structured screenplay/film has got content which helps give form, or shape, to a story.

More often than not, effective storytelling fully expresses its devastating potential in the pitch black of the editing room. Great film editors are masters of storytelling. They know how to recognise key turning points in the story they're telling and most of all how to make the most of them through the power of the images. Movies are primarily visual after all.

Let's have a look at some of the basic turning points which make a story move forward or "turn" into a new direction. The sooner we get familiar with the "skeleton", or the "structural model", the better.

1.1 • Catalyst

Definition:

Somewhere in the first 10 minutes of a movie, something should happen that gives the central character a goal, a desire, a mission, a need, or a problem to solve. When a story begins, life is in balance. Our hero may have a problem, but it's a problem they have always had.

Then *the Catalyst kicks things out of balance* and gives our central character a new need, goal or desire which makes them spend the rest of the movie getting things back into balance.

CATALYST

Player 'A', Maximus, is arrested by the Praetorian guard, 'B', and is told that he and his family will die.

Maximus must pay the price for refusing to show his loyalty to the Emperor Commodus.

1.2 • Big event

Definition:

The second major turning point in a movie, is called Big event because it dramatically affects the central character's life. The main idea this big change revolves around, is similar to the Catalyst, giving the character a new goal or need. However, there's a huge difference between the two: while the Catalyst kicks things out of balance without making our hero embark immediately on a journey to achieve his new goal, the Big event is what finally *pushes them,* reluctantly or not, *to set out on a new path.*

BIG EVENT

Player 'A', Kubo, gets separated from his mother, 'B', who uses her magic to send him far away.

Kubo must set off and find his father's armor.

1.3 • Pinch

Definition:

All great scripts have a beginning, middle and an end. Through Catalyst and Big event screenwriters and editors set up the story and grab people's attention. When the central character emerges from Act 1 with a desire to do something about the difficult situation created by the Big event, we're ready to move to the Pinch.

The Pinch is often *the point of no return.* A new change, need or conflict forces the hero to carry on on their path to achieve the final goal. They are fully committed and there's no way to go back to the beginning.

PINCH

Player 'A', Benjamin, reveals to Elaine, 'B', that the married woman he's had an affair with is her mother, Mrs Robinson.

Elaine is so upset that she refuses to see Benjamin again.

1.4 • Crisis

Definition:

There wouldn't be any drama without contrast, conflict or opposition. Movies would be emotionless and audiences would walk away from theatres. What's the worst thing that can happen to our hero? That's precisely what Crisis is about. The character faces *a crucial decision when everything seems lost.* They are overwhelmed by the course of events, hitting rock bottom, getting to the point where something must be done to get out of trouble.

The crisis is the moment where everything hangs in the balance in a state of being in which a pivotal change is about to happen. One decision is the difference between complete success and complete failure, between life and death, growth and defeat. It's basically the time where the hero needs to regroup and bounce back after slipping up.

CRISIS

Seeeking revenge, player 'B', Seol Hee, engages in a sword fight with Yoo Baek, player 'A'.

All seems lost as she gets severely wounded and defeated by the military ruler.

1.5 • Showdown

Definition:

Let's think of a Showdown as *the final face-off* in a good, old western between the bold outlaw and the corrupt Sheriff. It follows on the heels of the Crisis to bring the main character one step closer to the goal, which is finally on the line. This is the high point of a movie, *the Climax*, where the hero, based on what has been learned throughout the journey, determines what final action needs to be taken in order to resolve the conflict. There might be of course an inner conflict a well as an outer conflict affecting the hero and a good showdown is not necessarily about fighting a villain. Sometimes personal struggles and deep fears to overcome are far more dramatic than rifles and swords. What really counts is that any other series of events in the movie, lead up to the Showdown.

SHOWDOWN

Player 'A' and 'B', Mortimer and El Indio, are finally face to face, ready to engage in a pistol duel.

El Indio must pay for what he's done to Mortimer's sister.

1.6 • Realization

Definition:

After the climatic final scene of a movie, the central character usually realises something new about himself. The audience is shown that there's some visible or spoken *evidence of change and growth.* Our hero has been through a crucible and as a result of it we clearly understand that something has inevitably changed forever. We've seen the heroes sow the seeds of their own destruction, fall, cry, fight to the death, learn, grow, and eventually face their demons.

If there's no evidence of change in our hero, the whole point of embarking on a journey loses its dramatic power. From a storytelling point of view, "change" is the measure of how a character develops over time, from the very beginning all the way through to the end. A "flat" protagonist is a shallow character who doesn't care about inner growth, someone audiences will hardly ever relate to or empathise with.

REALIZATION

Player 'B', Mr Darcy, professes his love to Elizabeth, 'A', who finally accepts his proposal.

Elizabeth eventually finds out that her prejudice against Darcy was misplaced.

In a nutshell:

The Greek philosopher Aristotle wrote in his *Poetics* that all drama has a beginning, a middle and an end. Basic film structure follows that principle, therefore we can usually split a script/film into *"Three acts"*.

Act 1 = Catalyst and Big event.
Act 2 = Pinch and Crisis.
Act 3 = Showdown and Realization.

Those above are also called *"Turning points"* and they help the film-maker move from one part of the story to another. For example: the Big event is what moves the audience and the story from Act 1 to Act 2. The Crisis does the same, moving us from Act 2 to Act 3.

The "Three-act-structure" is by no means something you must stick with. You can have 4 Acts if you wish (Act 1, beginning, Act 2 and 3, middle, Act 4, end). Or perhaps 5. No matter how many Acts you go for, always plan ahead of time how your story is going to unfold. Hopefully before getting into the editing room!

PART
TWO

2

FILM EDITING TO THE RESCUE

Writing a script is undoubtedly the first step of the extremely long and exciting journey that brings a movie to life. When the screenwriter works on a great idea, which can stand on its own two legs, chances are good that the film will be successful. It's easier said than done. Movie history is packed with projects that didn't turn out well even if based on great concepts or screenplays. And we're not talking about super expensive movie flops, but promising projects that didn't live up to the audiences' expectations, regardless of the available budget. It is not uncommon for film editors to literally turn a script upside-down in the editing Room. Let's see first *what they usually look for* when comparing the script to the rushes/dailies[1] and then learn *how they come to the rescue* when the need arises.

---

1 Unedited, raw visual and sound footage from the day's shooting.

23

2.1 • Goal & Opposition

Definition:

When we are told a story, we unconsciously want to know two basic things: what action is going on and how people involved are reacting to that action. *Your characters want something.* This dramatic goal should be specific, clear and most of all not easy to attain. There must be opposition to the goal. Opposition creates conflict and conflict makes drama. When the editor leafs through the script, they need to make sure that those two key elements will be neatly conveyed to the audience.

GOAL & OPPOSITION

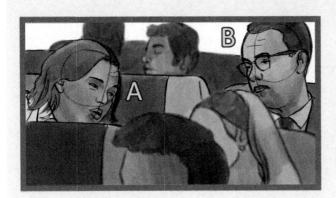

On the plane back to the US, the FBI agent Carl Hanratty, player 'B', informs Frank, 'A', that is father has died.

Grief-stricken Frank escapes from the plane to reach his mother's house.

2.2 • Motivation

Definition:

As a film-maker or editor you should always ask yourself this question: *why do my characters want what they want?* The answer is motivation. The more personal the motivation that pushes the characters, the better. Audiences will more easily identify with them, whether they're the hero or the villain. More often than not they are way more charismatic, smart and lively than their "good" counterparts. Great editors are aware that motivation only grows with conflict and often becomes most evident at the midpoint of a story. If the script lacks motivation, the editor must come up with an effective solution, like spreading clues throughout the movie that lead the audience to the hero's motivation.

MOTIVATION

Player 'A', William Wallace is giving a speech to the Scottish warrios to persuade them to fight the English.

In doing so he keeps his soldiers from retreating and gives them courage by inspiring them to value their freedom.

2.3 ● Backstory

Definition:

Before page one on any script, something significant happened to the central character. That singular and *life changing event* is called backstory. Sometimes only the screenwriter knows the backstory and thanks to that knowledge the character gains dramatic depth. When the backstory is not shown to the audience and the editor feels that there's something missing on screen, it's time to introduce sequences or flashbacks that unveil what haunts and motivates our hero's actions.

BACKSTORY

Player 'A', Spooner, finally reveals to Susan Calvin, a character off screen, the truth about his past.

The confession sheds light on why Spooner distrusts and hates robots so much.

2.4 • Will to act

Definition:

How do we usually judge a person? By words or by actions? Probably both. However, movies thrive on action and directors and editors are fully aware of that. Dialogue can tell us a lot, but what really makes a story engaging is that exciting moment when *the central character eventually takes action and reveals his true colours.* A person does what they do because of who they are and when the script is too dialogue-driven, it's time for the editor to be as "visual" as possible and "show" what the script only "tells". This is undoubtedly one of the more relevant differences between script and rushes/dailies. Part of what is written is always left to the reader's imagination. They'll picture the hero or the villain the way they think they should look, regardless of any physical descriptions contained within the script. But things change radically once the audiences have someone right in front of their eyes. The same goes with "reading" about actions and "watching" them on the big screen.

WILL TO ACT

Player 'A', Chief, has had enough of the tyrannical nurse in charge of the Mental Institution in which he's locked up.

It's time to smash the window gates and escape from that terrible place.

2.5 • The power of editing

Definition:

Unfortunately sometimes things don't go as planned. There might be countless reasons why a good script won't turn into a great movie if the footage is not handled properly in the editing room. Often what works on paper doesn't really deliver on the screen and solutions must be found to work out the issue and get the movie back on track. Editing can be compared to plumbing: you take two shots and put them together. If you do it right then water flows through. It's basically the combination of different images which gives the audience the thrill they crave when watching a movie. The editor is responsible for telling a story, no matter how good the footage they are working with can be. There's always the chance to get a nicely edited scene out of mediocre material. Creativity and open-mindedness are key factors in being effective while doing so.

2.6 ● Teamwork

Definition:

Let's not forget though, that film-making ultimately is a team effort. An editor who's not comfortable in working with other people usually doesn't have great chances of being successful at what he/she does. Especially when it comes to collaborating with directors. It's great for an editor to be involved in the storytelling of a film and bring ideas to the table, but always without losing sight of what the role entails. If the director doesn't like a certain idea it's pivotal to give them time to process the information and go back to it much further down the line (a week or a month later), when because of new decisions made in the editing room, that rejected idea suddenly looks more valuable than it was when presented for the first time. Editors must support directors and help them look with different eyes at scenes or sequences they have trouble with. I've witnessed myself more than once, how a bland scene can get turned into a well shaped piece of work. All thanks to a close partnership with the director and an open and honest exchange of ideas about the movie. When two people work together and care about the film, there's nothing to difficult to do, nor hurdle which can't be overcome.

2.7 ● Less is more

Definition:

It's very hard when you have a good film and for one reason or another you have *to drop a scene*, remove a few lines or cut it down to a specific length. Editors deal with those issues on a daily basis and the sooner you learn how to cope with your unpleasant feelings about the whole matter, the better. We have to do what we have to do. Part of the job is to make sure that the movie has a good dramatic structure, isn't exceedingly long and has flow and pace to entertain and keep the audience engaged. Sometimes it takes days or weeks to bring a scene down to the right length, often fighting with the director over some lines to cut out or a few more frames to shave off. As the great Walter Murch puts it: *"It's like being on a hot-air balloon which is about to crash. What do you do? You start throwing things overboard to give you more lift".*

2.8 ● Restructuring

Definition:

It's not uncommon to hear writers complain about how their script got turned into an unrecognisable movie. What comes out of the editing room, I dare say, at least 50% of the time (perhaps even more) is "something else" compared to the script. How to forget Ring Lardner Jr.'s reaction to the final cut of the black comedy M*A*S*H (1970, directed by Robert Altman). He was livid about the changes made to his script and could only be consoled by winning an Academy Award for best adapted screenplay (MASH was based on Richard Hooker's 1968 novel *MASH: A Novel About Three Army Doctors*).

No matter how good a script can be, there are all kinds of alterations to it made in the editing room in the effort to keep the flow going or make something on the screen clearer which wasn't on the page. Editors usually say that the "film talks to them". That, I believe, is true. The film emerges on the screen, restructuring it is part of the game and as film-makers and editors we must always be aware of the ultimate goal of a successful production: trying to get the best possible film out of the available footage.

2.9 ● Dry-cutting

Definition:

I could potentially spend dozens of pages on this particular subject as it's been part of my editing philosophy for as long as I can remember. The thing is, cutting a scene or a sequence without music, almost certainly helps the editor get the pace right without any kind of external distraction. Sticking temp-tracks on your first cuts is a huge pitfall. Most often what is pushing the scene is the track, rather than good storytelling and pace. It's the rhythm of the images which really counts. You can play with it, increasing it or slowing it down, but you must not lose sight of what drives the story forward. We all know that when music is involved everything gets better. The point of dry-cutting is taking the film to a level where it works within your timeline, before the music boost is added. Mind you, I'm not suggesting to never use temp-tracks. It can be done perhaps when dealing with montage sequences or once a rough cut is completed and ready to be delivered to the director or the production in order to make it more "watchable". But still, the best way to put an edit together should be by letting it rely on its internal pace, flow and rhythm. Once again: the rhythm of the images is what really counts.

2.10 ● Risk-taking

Definition:

Last but not least on *how editors come to the rescue when a film is not yet in the right place:* risk-taking. It sounds crazy but it is not uncommon for an editor to get stuck at a crossroads unable to choose whether to take the story into a certain direction as opposed to another. Movies can go wrong for all kinds of reasons.

A good editor has got *that gut feeling which helps capitalise on mistakes* made during the shooting, such as missing scenes, continuity issues, technical problems and so on. I'm not saying that we should all be able to work as the Japanese director Takeshi Kitano does, by *"shooting in a hurry in order to not waste the thrilling feeling of fixing something in the edit"*, but still a certain dose of risk taking is a relevant part of each production and simply cannot be avoided. The difficult bit is being able to put into words and explain to others why you "feel" that something is "right".

✂ PART THREE

3

KEY ELEMENTS OF FILM DIALOGUE

Movie making is a craft that thrives on action. The power and flow created by sequences of music and images is undoubtedly part of the successful recipe that keeps audiences glued to their seats. However, there are many ways to tell the same story and sometimes great dialogue can be a powerful means to communicate feelings and emotions otherwise hard to get across through action.

Editing plays a crucial role when it comes to determining how dialogue should be implemented in the main story-line, and most of all when it shouldn't, letting the characters' actions speak for them. Let's take a look at some key elements of film dialogue, editors should always take into account when cutting a scene.

3.1 • Style

Definition:

The way a person speaks, often determines who the person is. Styles may differ from one another, but in movies they always serve the same purpose, to tell the characters apart. The range of possibilities is huge: from mumbling to discursive, flowery to ponderous, a certain style makes a character stand out and stick in the audiences' minds straight away. Editors often take advantage of such a powerful tool and carefully administer the lines of dialogue in order to create the right balance between too little and too much.

3.2 ● Subtext

Definition:
It's not what you say, but how you say it. Deep dialogue is what lies under the writer's text. Something hidden between the lines, the real content of the words, what they really mean. *Characters should never say exactly what they feel.* We need to understand the emotion going on within them, through actions, storytelling and subtext. Audiences must be guided step by step to the motivations that drive the character's actions, avoiding revealing them all at once.

Once again, regardless of the script, it's the editor's job, often along with the director, to find the proper context to one or more lines of dialogue within a scene or a sequence. What was originally conceived as "literal language" can easily be turned into subtext if the words are properly handled.

3.3 ● Accent

Definition:
There's probably nothing more distinctive than your character's accent. Accent can immediately trigger a social categorisation in an unconscious manner. We might even judge a person based just on their accent. Movies aim at creating contrast, opposition and most of all emotions. A proper use of the character's accent can efficiently serve all these purposes at once.
There's no doubt that accent is a fascinating and powerful tool for writers and editors, as it has a meaningful impact on the way we interpret the world around us.

3.4 ● Slang

Definition:
Generally speaking, dialogue should never be real-life speech. There's a significant difference between the way people speak in real life and in movies. The screenwriter's text is usually deprived of anything extraneous to the words themselves, such as hesitations and interruptions.

However, there's an exception to this rule: slang. Slang can often be a smart way to give depth and believability to a single individual or group, making them stand out from the rest of the characters. It is also a double-edged sword. Too much slang within a scene might easily throw people off, breaking the film's flow and making the audience lose interest in the main narrative. To a certain degree this type of issue is similar to "mumble acting", which has the main purpose to make scenes more realistic through a whispered style of acting, which more often than not doesn't really achieve the desired effect. Be careful when dealing with slang.

3.5 ● Rhythm

Definition:

One must-know rule about dialogue, that editors are fully aware of, is that *exposition possesses a rhythm of its own.* Like a musical score, the way a characters speaks, in terms of rhythm, can drastically change between one and another, adding subtle nuances to the construction of a hero or a villain.

Sometimes, we get attracted to a character thanks to the way they wait before answering a question, or delivering a line, fascinated also by the sound of their voice, by the pulse which lies behind the lines of dialogue (*"This is Sparta"*; *"At my signal, unleash Hell"*; *"I am your father"*). And whether characters should always have their own particular speaking rhythm to affect the audiences' emotional response to them, those who can turn that rhythm into a dialogue resembling a "music sheet", are the editors. A few frames added or a few frames removed from a shot might make the difference between a plain dialogue and a powerful, flawless, "musical" one.

Pace and rhythm, combined with music of course, are potentially the most relevant and decisive elements that contribute to take a film to a different level of dramatic weight. I can easily think, off the top of my head, of at least a few amazing examples of impeccable achievements obtained by film-makers and editors who nailed the perfect mix of pace and rhythm, combined with music and dialogue:

1) The opening scene in the *The Godfather (1972)*.
2) The final pistol duel between Lord Bullingdon and Redmond Barry in Stanley Kubrick's masterpiece *Barry Lyndon (1975)*.

3) The final chase scene in *The Last of the Mohicans (1992)*.

4) The "Funny how?" scene in *GoodFellas (1990)*.

5) The "Pikey caravan" scene in *Snatch (2000)*.

6) The "Say what again" scene in *Pulp Fiction (1994)*.

7) The "Over the line" scene from *The Big Lebowski (1998)*.

8) William Wallace motivational speech to the Scots in *Braveheart (1995)*.

PART
FOUR

4

FILM-MAKING BASIC TOOLS

Each craft has a basic body of rules and principles which help the craftsman understand what they're doing throughout the creative process. If you don't even know how to use a chisel I'll find it hard to believe you'll ever be able to achieve great woodcarving. The same goes with film-making. Whether you like it or not our craft requires each professional to grasp at least the basics of any other film department (writing, cinematography, camera work, directing, sound design, editing and so on).

If you are not willing to bother putting yourself in other people's shoes, chances are you'll end up being an industry "lone wolf" someone who goes by their own rules without being able to see the "bigger picture" and be a cog in the wheel. Film-making is – and always will be – a collaborative process. In order to bring a movie to life, cast and crew work toward an explicit goal, difficult enough to inspire them, but not so unreachable that the team becomes dispirited. Every individual normally posses technical and artistic skills which enable them to work alongside dozens if not hundreds of professionals at the same time, in a coordinated effort to achieve the best possible result. There is no way around it, destructive team dynamics can quickly undermine collaborative efforts, especially when team members come from different experiences and backgrounds.

4.1 ● The 180-Degree rule

Definition:

It's a basic film-making rule created to keep screen direction, preserve continuity of movement and match eyelines.

How it works:

Draw an imaginary line – called the *Line of interest* – between two players/actors, place your camera on one side of the line and stick to it. When dealing with a single player/actor, *the direction in which they are looking*, sets the line.

Shooting plan:

The direction in which the actor looks, governs the line of interest. The camera is always placed on the same side of the imaginary 180-degree arc that surrounds the player. When the camera is placed right over the line of interest, overlapping it, that position is called the *"neutral position".*

As long as the shot you're editing into a sequence *doesn't completely cross the line*, you'll be fine and the continuity of movement will always be preserved. In the example below, player **'A'**, Arthur (Matthew McConaughey), is trekking into a forest called Aokigahara, consistently walking from right to left across the frame (apart from cam-1 and cam-3 which are neutral shots).

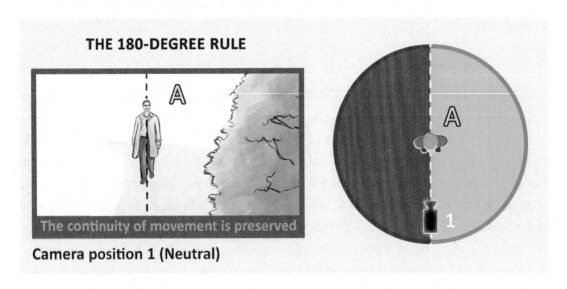

THE 180-DEGREE RULE

The continuity of movement is preserved

Camera position 1 (Neutral)

THE 180-DEGREE RULE

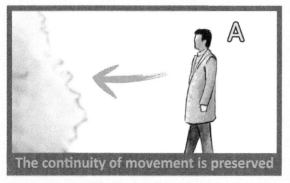

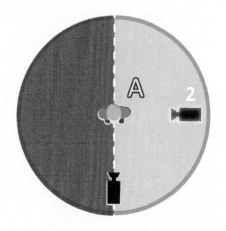

Camera position 2 (Right-Left)

THE 180-DEGREE RULE

Camera position 3 (Neutral)

THE 180-DEGREE RULE

Camera position 2 (Right-Left)

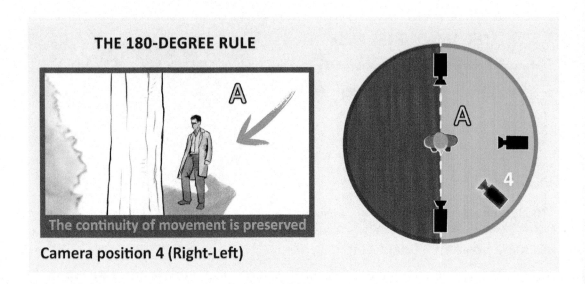

THE 180-DEGREE RULE

The continuity of movement is preserved

Camera position 4 (Right-Left)

In a nutshell:

Green side of the line = The camera should stay on this side to preserve visual consistency. Same goes into the editing room. You should only use shots taken from the green side of the line, unless you cross the line properly through a cut-away or showing the change of line on screen (see chapter 6.4).

Red side of the line = As a rule of thumb, the camera should never stay on this side. Sticking to this rule ensures to avoid conflicting directions of movement on screen, which means a player walking from screen-right to screen-left in one shot and from screen-left to screen-right in another (therefore into opposite directions. Extremely confusing to the audience). The editor should always be aware of the importance of the continuity of movement on the screen.

Once again, we're talking about basic principles which have exceptions, but we'll see what those exceptions are after laying the groundwork. Let's take a look at what happens when you shoot – and later on cut one after the other, back-to-back – two angles from opposite sides of the line of interest (following picture). As you can see, player **'A'** ends up walking from right to left in shot 1 and from left to right in shot 2.

THE 180-DEGREE RULE

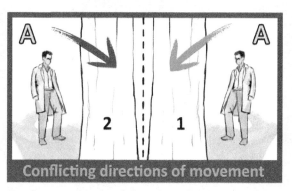

Conflicting directions of movement

Both camera positions at the same time

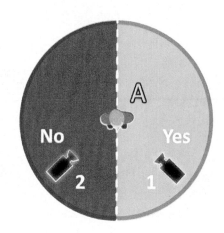

4.2 ● The "Triangle" principle

Definition:

First application of the 180-Degree rule. It's used to cover two players/actors placed on the same side of the line of interest. The basic setup is obtained by placing the *cameras in a triangular arrangement.*

How it works:

Cam-1 covers player **'B'**, cam-2 player **'A'**, cam-3 takes a master shot with both players within the shot.

Shooting plan:

When two players are facing each other, it's quite easy to draw the line of interest running between them. *The position of the heads is crucial.* The position of the bodies doesn't matter. Human bodies can assume many positions. *We need a point of reference to draw the line of interest and that point is the players' heads.*

In a nutshell:

Follow the 180-Degree rule to ensure that the players stay on the same side of the screen no matter which position of the camera you switch to. As you can see player **'A'** is always positioned on the left side of the screen while **'B'** is on the right.

THE "TRIANGLE" PRINCIPLE

 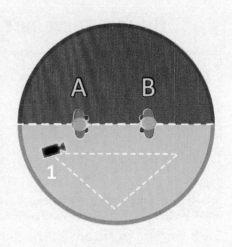

Camera position 1

THE "TRIANGLE" PRINCIPLE

 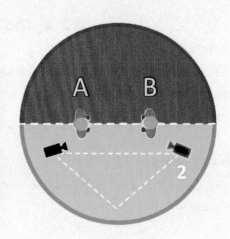

Camera position 2

THE "TRIANGLE" PRINCIPLE

 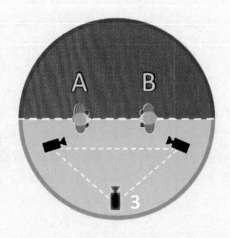

Camera position 3

4.3 ● Basic camera arrangements

Definition:

A scene involving at least two players/actors can be covered using *5 basic camera arrangements*. Each variant follows the triangle principle and entails a direct application of it. Let's take a look at each one of them individually. Always bear in mind that you can choose *only one side of the line of interest* when placing the cameras.

EXTERNAL REVERSE ANGLES
(Camera arrangement 1)

INTERNAL REVERSE ANGLES
(Camera arrangement 2)

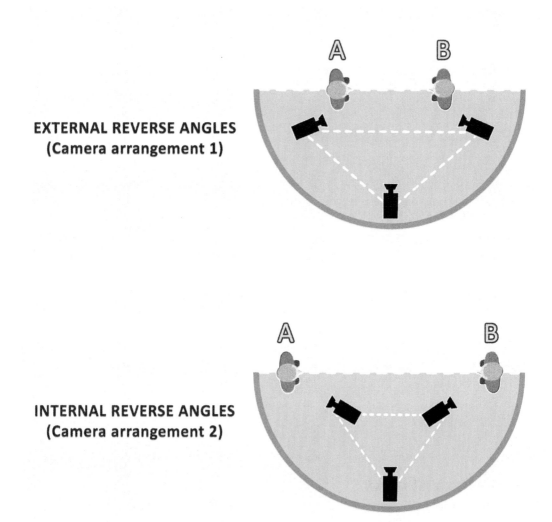

PARALLEL POSITIONS
(Camera arrangement 3)

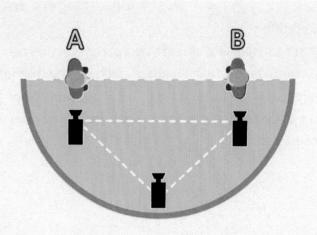

RIGHT ANGLE
(Camera arrangement 4)

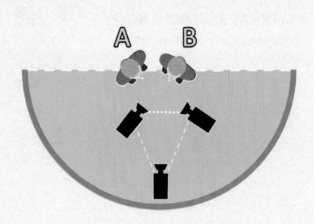

COMMON VISUAL AXIS
(Camera arrangement 5)

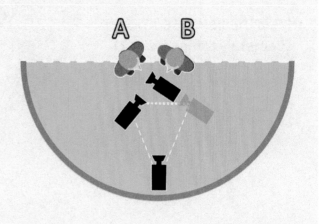

Take a careful look at the previous camera arrangements. In the following chapter we'll see how to use them to cover a dialogue scene involving two players. It goes without saying (that's why I'm saying it) that you don't necessarily need to shoot a dialogue scene keeping three or more cameras running on set at the same time. Based on the size of the production, budget or time constraints, you might want to shoot one angle at the time and afterwards send everything over to the film editors, who are going to bang their heads against a brick wall, trying to match the shots with each other, while at the same time keeping the continuity and flow of the edit intact.

PART
FIVE

5

DIALOGUE: TWO PLAYERS/ACTORS

Static dialogue scenes represent the most basic way to approach film-making. On a small scale production this type of scene usually gets shot multiple times from multiple different angles, to add variety to the coverage and leave more options to the editor. On big productions the crew can have multiple cameras rolling at the same time. No matter the budget, the pitfalls and challenges of static dialogue are pretty much the same: trying to keep the audience engaged and focused on the story unfolding on the screen while at the same time there's little or no movement happening within the filmic space (even though when the cameras are static, normally the actors do move slightly from time to time).

Movement also helps hiding mistakes. It is way easier to spot a continuity issue in a static dialogue scene than in a super hectic car chasing sequence. Think of that glass of wine being half empty in a shot, full in the next one and completely empty in the last (that's gonna bother the director, trust me). So despite being a very basic means to tell a story, static dialogue does require a fair dose of filming experience to be mastered. Let's see why.

5.1 ● Face to face

Definition:

Two players/actors standing or sitting before each other, face to face, in linear arrangement. Widely considered the *most popular approach* to static dialogue scenes.

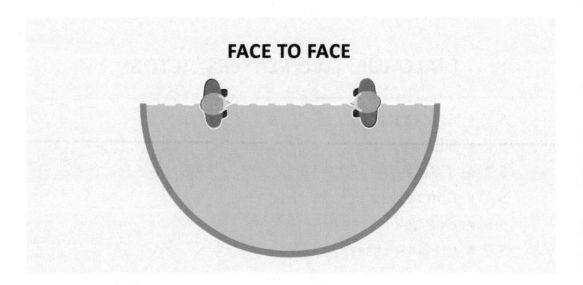

How it works:

There are *three main camera arrangements* employed to cover this kind of scene:

→ EXTERNAL REVERSE ANGLES

→ EXTERNAL + INTERNAL REVERSE ANGLES

→ INTERNAL REVERSE ANGLES

Shooting plan:

Static dialogue scenes face to face, usually lead to iterative editing patterns: back and forth from cam-1, to cam-2. Therefore the pattern would be 1-2-1-2. The combination of an external and an internal reverse camera position, creates *number contrast* on the screen (which means that we see both players in one shot and only one of them in the other).

EXTERNAL REVERSE ANGLES
(Camera arrangement 1)

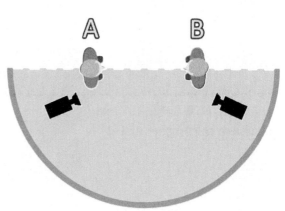

EXTERNAL REVERSE ANGLES
(Camera arrangement 1)

Camera position 1

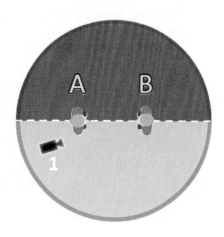

EXTERNAL REVERSE ANGLES
(Camera arrangement 1)

Camera position 2

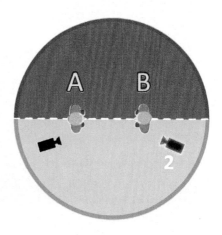

EXTERNAL/INTERNAL REVERSE
(Camera arrangement 2)

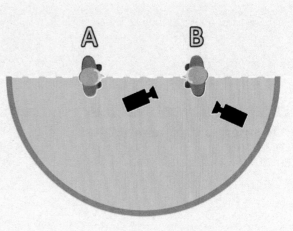

EXTERNAL/INTERNAL REVERSE ANGLES
(Camera arrangement 2)

Camera position 1

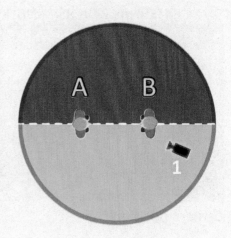

EXTERNAL/INTERNAL REVERSE ANGLES
(Camera arrangement 2)

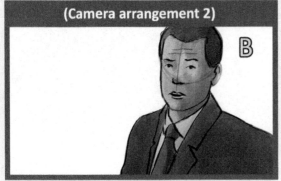

Camera position 2

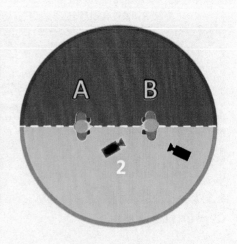

INTERNAL REVERSE ANGLES
(Camera arrangement 3)

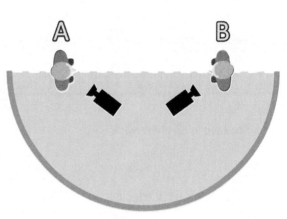

INTERNAL REVERSE ANGLES
(Camera arrangement 3)

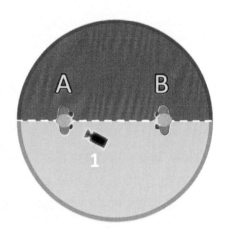

Camera position 1

INTERNAL REVERSE ANGLES
(Camera arrangement 3)

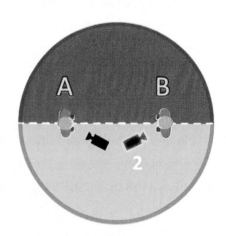

Camera position 2

In a nutshell:

Green side of the line = Iterative editing pattern: 1-2-1-2. Player **'A'** and **'B'**, always keep their screen positions from shot to shot.

Red side of the line = As a rule of thumb, don't use shots taken from the red side of the line of interest. If you fail to stick to this principle, player **'A'** and **'B'** will switch screen sides from shot to shot, creating a confusing editing pattern to the audience.

FAQ:

Q = How can we add variety to a 1-2-1-2 editing pattern when there's not enough coverage?

A = Timing is the key. If you haven't got any additional angle available, try to vary the interval between cuts.

Q = What if the additional angles available have been taken from the wrong side of the line of interest?

A = The most basic solution to fix the issue is to insert a neutral shot or a cut-away before the angle which crosses the line (see chapter 6.4).

Q = How much importance should we give to continuity mistakes? Also, what counts more within a scene, continuity or overall flow and performance?

A = Continuity mistakes do have the potential to affect the way a scene is edited. The editor might be tempted to discard a shot just because the actor's arm position is not the same as in the previous shot. This attitude often leads to scenes impeccable from a continuity point of view but lacking in pace, emotion and rhythm. I personally believe that the final goal of a film-maker is to create an engaging scene, not a technically perfect one (not exclusively at least).

5.2 ● Side by side

Definition:

Two players standing or sitting next to each other, side by side, in linear arrangement. This shooting technique is widely employed to cover *car scenes,* where the characters' positions inside the vehicle are forced by the presence of the seats.

SIDE BY SIDE

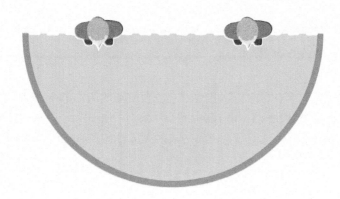

How it works:

There are *three main camera arrangements* employed to cover this kind of scene:

→ EXTERNAL REVERSE ANGLES

→ INTERNAL REVERSE ANGLES

→ PARALLEL CAMERAS

Shooting plan:

Two players placed side by side usually look forward, in the same North-South direction. Yet the line of interest still runs "across" their heads in an East-West direction. The new line, North-South, is called the *line of action.*

LINE OF ACTION (N-S) - LINE OF INTEREST (E-W)

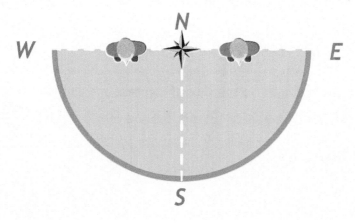

Line of action:

It's the line which *follows the direction of motion inside the screen.* Sometimes this line can coexist with the line of interest inside the same scene. The most common case in which they coexist, is when we cut a sequence that involves passengers riding in a vehicle of any sort.

As we can see from the picture below, even though the **line of interest** runs in an **East-West direction** between the players' heads, the other line – the **line of action** – runs **North-South** outside the car and follows the direction of motion inside the screen.

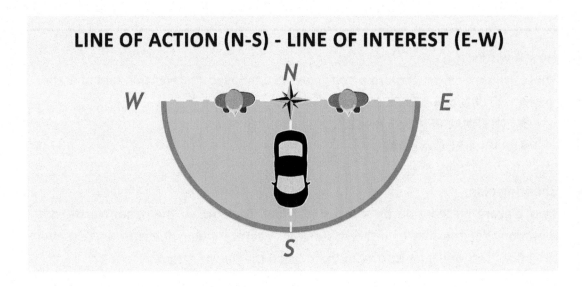

In a nutshell:

Green = East-West direction: Line of interest

Red = North-South: Line of action (often vehicle movement).

Now that we have shed light on the **line of interest** and the **line of action**, let's go back to the three camera arrangements used to cover a dialogue between two players sitting or standing side by side, regardless of whether they are placed inside a vehicle, riding or driving one.

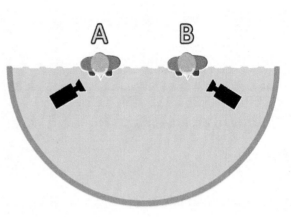

EXTERNAL REVERSE ANGLES
(Camera arrangement 1)

Camera position 1

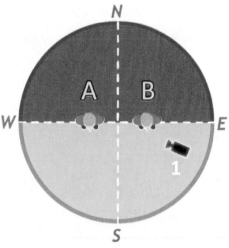

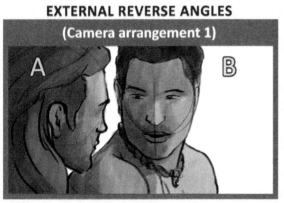

Camera position 2

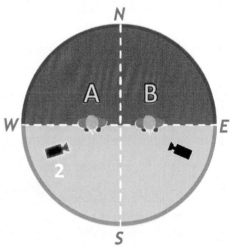

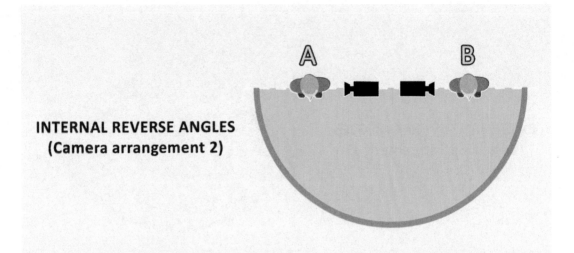

INTERNAL REVERSE ANGLES
(Camera arrangement 2)

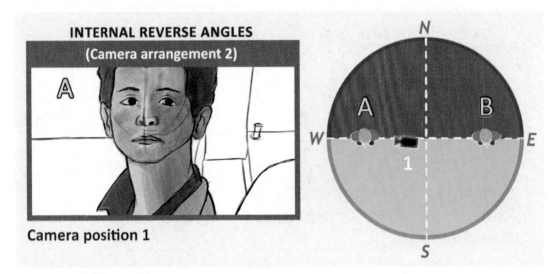

Camera position 1

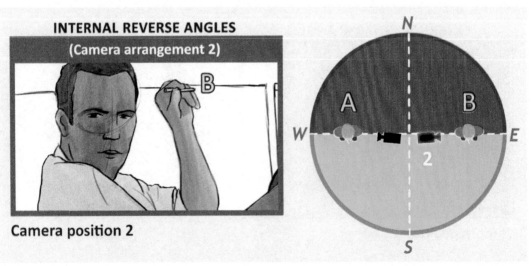

Camera position 2

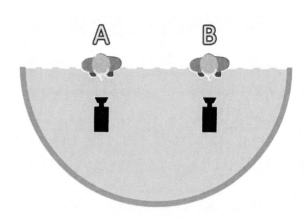

PARALLEL CAMERAS
(Camera arrangement 3)

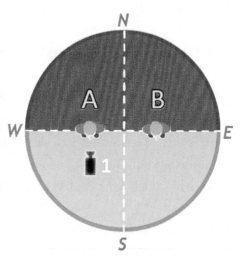

PARALLEL CAMERAS
(Camera arrangement 3)

Camera position 1

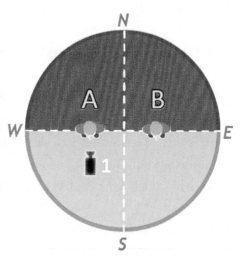

PARALLEL CAMERAS
(Camera arrangement 3)

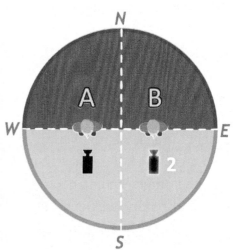

Camera position 2

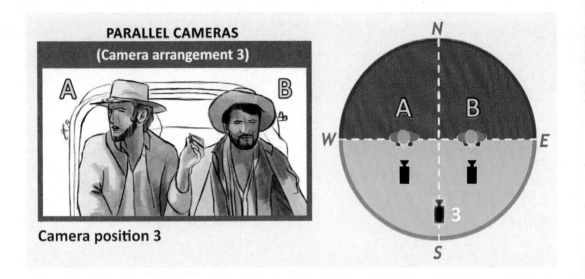

Camera position 3

FAQ:

Q = In the second example (cam arrangement 2), each time we switch to a different camera position the background moves into opposite directions, from screen-left to screen-right (cam-1) and from screen-right to screen-left (cam-2). Isn't the **line of action** making us break the 180-Degree rule?

A = The line of action runs North-South, following the natural movement of a vehicle on screen. But what really counts in a side by side dialogue scene is the **line of interest**, which runs East-West, between the players (See chapters 4.2 and 5.2).

Q = What if the players are not inside a vehicle but are riding a horse or driving a carriage? What happens to the line of interest and the line of action?

A = In those cases, since we can see the players' bodies and there's no way to hide their presence inside a vehicle, switching between both lines depends on what takes priority within the sequence. If preserving the direction and continuity of motion inside the screen is crucial, then of course we'll stick as much as possible to the line of action. Think about a carriage driving "in town" following a movement on the screen from right to left and "out of town" following a movement from left to right. The audience will assume where the players are going based on the direction in which the vehicle is moving on the screen.

If, on the other hand, it doesn't matter in which direction the carriage is moving because the story itself is moving forward and what counts is the current "turning point", then the line of action can be disregarded.

5.3 ● Right angle

Definition:

Two players standing or sitting close to each other in a right angle position. The definition also refers to a camera set-up, therefore two cameras can be placed in a right angle position too.

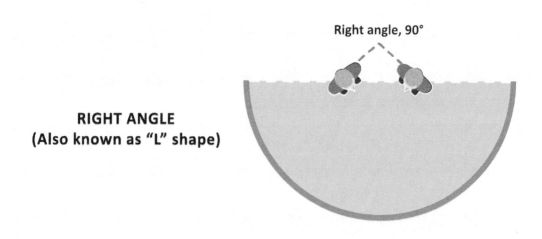

RIGHT ANGLE
(Also known as "L" shape)

How it works:

There are *several camera arrangements* employed to cover this kind of scene:

→ EXTERNAL REVERSE ANGLES
   - Face inwards
   - Back to back
   - Face outwards

→ EXTERNAL REVERSE + INTERNAL ANGLES
   - Face inwards
   - Back to back
   - Face outwards

Shooting plan:

A right angle camera position is usually employed when both players adopt a right angle body rapport. However, that kind of "L" formation *doesn't have to be covered exclusively by a right angle camera deployment.*

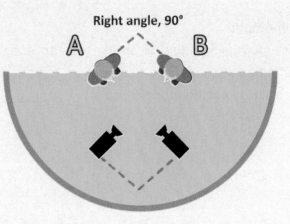

EXTERNAL REVERSE ANGLES
Face inwards
(Camera arrangement 1)

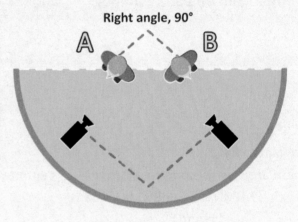

EXTERNAL REVERSE ANGLES
Back to back
(Camera arrangement 2)

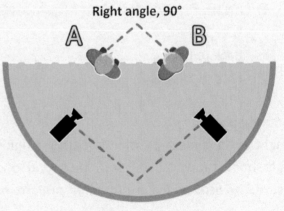

EXTERNAL REVERSE ANGLES
Face outwards
(Camera arrangement 3)

EXTERNAL REVERSE + INTERNAL
Face inwards
(Camera arrangement 4)

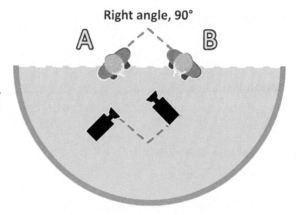

EXTERNAL REVERSE + INTERNAL
Back to back
(Camera arrangement 5)

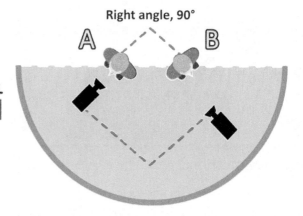

EXTERNAL REVERSE + INTERNAL
Face outwards
(Camera arrangement 6)

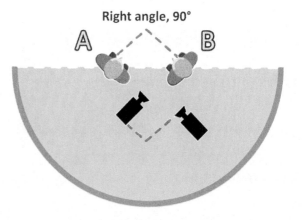

Let's now take a look at some examples taken from actual movies and TV series, which focus on camera arrangements 1, 2 and 3 only. These are usually the most popular so they're easy to come by.

In a nutshell:

Green side of the line = Right angle (both, cameras and bodies).

Red side of the line = As a rule of thumb, avoid cutting to shots taken from the red side of the line of interest.

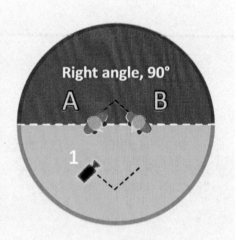

Camera position 1

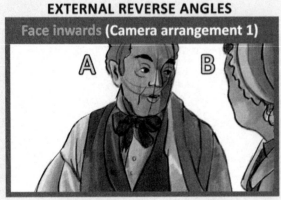

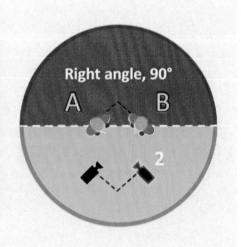

Camera position 2

EXTERNAL REVERSE ANGLES

Back to back (Camera arrangement 2)

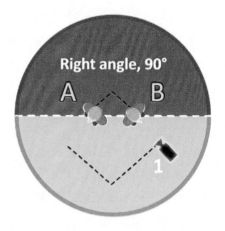

Camera position 1

EXTERNAL REVERSE ANGLES

Face outwards (Camera arrangement 3)

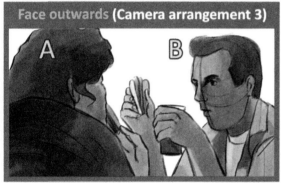

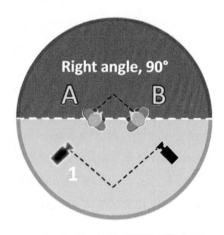

Camera position 1

EXTERNAL REVERSE ANGLES

Face outwards (Camera arrangement 3)

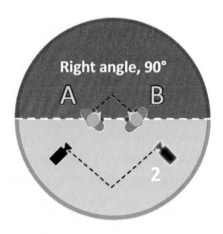

Camera position 2

FAQ:

Q = Does the body rapport between two players affect the way we cut from one shot to another in a static dialogue scene?

A = Potentially yes. There are several cases in which an unusual body position might lead to an "acceptable violation" of the 180-Degree rule. (Players hugging each other is the most popular one. See chapter 5.6).

Q = What should the editor do when coming across one of those unusual cases?

A = As a rule of thumb, the best workaround is to follow one of the basic editing patterns we've seen so far. However some "irregular cases" will be discussed in detail in chapter 5.6.

Q = Does the body rapport between two players within a shot affect the emotional experience of the audience?

A = Yes, it does. That's why *staging* and *blocking* are so important in film language. The former, in simple words, refers to where the camera will be placed on set, the latter to how the actors will move in front of it. Staging is a plan that often determines the work of hundreds of people on set, from the cinematographer to the set designer and the make-up artist. Staging is a craft in itself and requires years of practise and hard work to be honed. Akira Kurosawa (*Ran, Kagemusha*), Stanley Kubrick *(Paths of Glory, A Clockwork Orange)* and Alfred Hitchcock *(Vertigo)* were undoubtedly masters of staging.

Body language is a minefield that can easily turn into a nightmare on set if not handled properly. Even though generally speaking people tend to focus on the actors' faces, more than their bodies, the range of nonverbal signals that a specific body position delivers can easily clash with what the character is trying to express on an emotional level. A sloppy blocking leads to unnecessary and distracting movement within the frame, which often makes the audience disconnect from the story and disengage, losing interest in what's happening on the screen.

Camera arrangement 3 is a great example of effective blocking. The audience can easily figure out away why '**A**' is leaning over the table almost "offering" herself to '**B**', who's leisurely trying to eat a sandwich. The body rapport between the players serves the purpose of creating a nice contrast within the scene.

5.4 • Different camera heights

Definition:

Camera height influences the composition of any shot. Different heights are usually chosen to serve different purposes. As a rule of thumb, we can say that a *low-angle* shot makes the player look *strong and powerful*, while a *high-angle* shot achieves *the opposite* effect.

DIFFERENT CAMERA HEIGHTS

Low camera angle

High camera angle

How it works:

Sometimes different camera heights have the only purpose of accommodating the *different heights of the players/actors*. Let's analyse the most popular cases.

→ CHILD vs ADULT

→ SITTING vs STANDING

→ LYING NEXT TO EACH OTHER

Shooting plan:

As film-makers and video editors we must be aware of how *different heights* and angles *convey different messages to the audience,* in order to choose the shots that work best from a continuity and narrative point of view. If the camera tilt is too "extreme" the effect can be perceived as unreal. Normally we don't look at other people from such low or high viewpoints, therefore those angles should be used sparingly and only when serving a specific purpose.

CHILD vs ADULT
(Case 1)

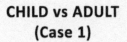

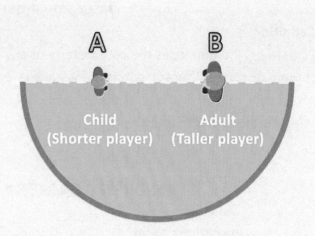

Child
(Shorter player)

Adult
(Taller player)

Camera position 1

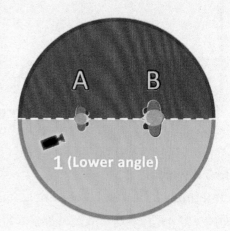

1 (Lower angle)

Camera position 2

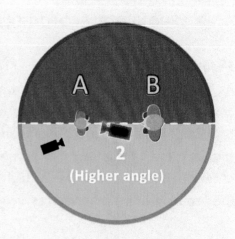

2
(Higher angle)

SITTING vs STANDING (Case 2)

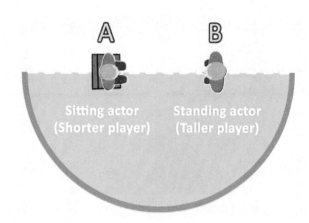

Sitting actor (Shorter player) Standing actor (Taller player)

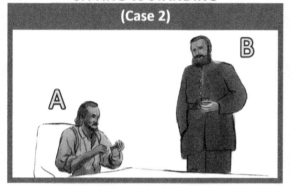

SITTING vs STANDING (Case 2)

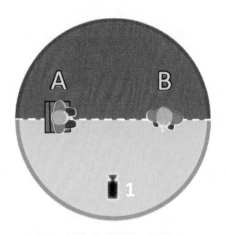

Camera position 1

SITTING vs STANDING (Case 2)

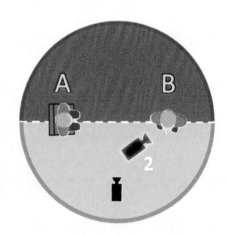

Camera position 2

SITTING vs STANDING
(Case 2)

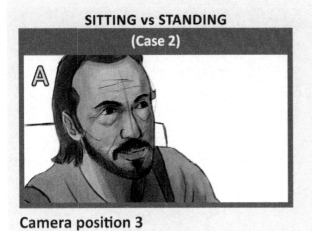

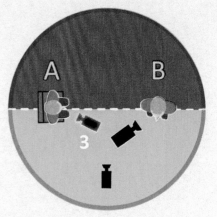

Camera position 3

LYING NEXT TO EACH OTHER
(Case 3)

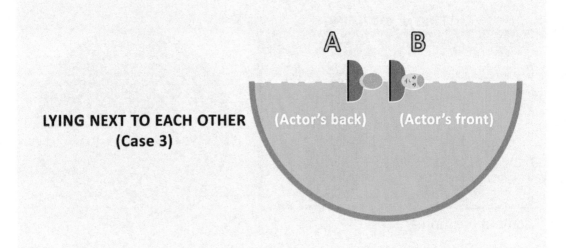

(Actor's back)   (Actor's front)

LYING NEXT TO EACH OTHER
(Case 3)

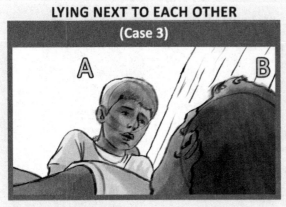

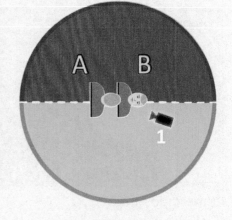

Camera position 1

LYING NEXT TO EACH OTHER
(Case 3)

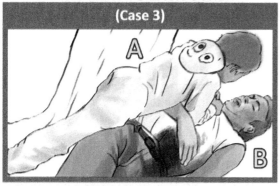

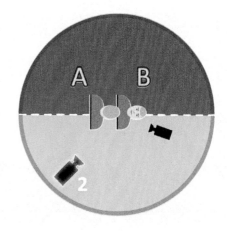

Camera position 2

LYING NEXT TO EACH OTHER
(Case 3)

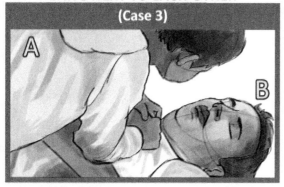

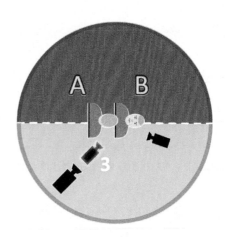

Camera position 3

EXTRA:

Trunk shot = An extremely popular type of shot achieved thanks to a low-angle camera position. It's also a "compartment shot", since usually the camera is placed within a container opened from the inside.

Let's take a look at one of the most iconic examples of a trunk shot, from Quentin Tarantino's *Reservoir dogs (1992).*

TRUNK SHOT

Player 'A', 'B' and 'C', Mr Blonde, Mr White and Mr Pink, are standing over the camera looking down at the car's boot.

Their demeanour and body positions deliver an utter feeling of dominance to the audience.

Fill, reveal frame = The trunk shot technique is extremely useful in editing, since it can be easily exploited to get a seamless type of cut called "Fill, reveal frame". When an object obscures the camera's view, the editor cuts to a new "dark" shot taken from a different angle.

A great example of this type of technique can be found in Hitchcock's *North by Northwest (1959),* at around 00:45:28. If you fancy looking for a few more cases yourself[2], here are some additional films where a **fill, reveal frame** has been used:

    1) *A Monster Calls (2016)*
    2) *Blow (2001)*
    3) *Crimson Peak (2015)*
    4) *Mayhem (2017)*
    5) *The Big Swindle (2004)*

---

2 By analysing movies you can learn a lot about film-making.

5.5 • One behind the other

Definition:

Two players *standing, sitting or riding a vehicle*, one behind the other. They are usually placed in linear arrangement while delivering their lines.

ONE BEHIND THE OTHER

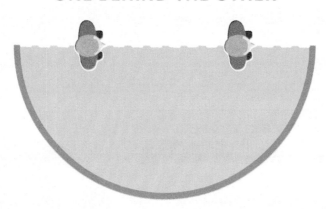

How it works:

There are *two main camera arrangements* employed to cover this kind of scene. Let's analyse each of them individually.

→ EXTERNAL REVERSE ANGLES
→ PARALLEL CAMERAS

Shooting plan:

When the players are conversing from that forced position – one behind the other – *the character in front* usually *turns his head* to look at the other one from the corner of their eye.

In a nutshell:

Green side of the line = Player 'B' turns her head to look at 'A'. This film-making conventional rule helps to get the audience focused on the dialogue scene showing on the screen.

Red side of the line = As a rule of thumb, avoid cutting to shots taken from the red side of the line of interest.

EXTERNAL REVERSE ANGLES
(Camera arrangement 1)

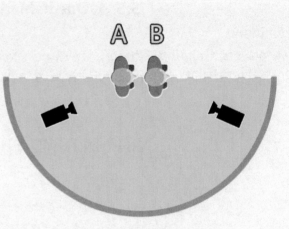

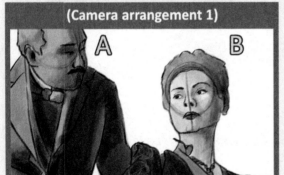

EXTERNAL REVERSE ANGLES
(Camera arrangement 1)

Camera position 1

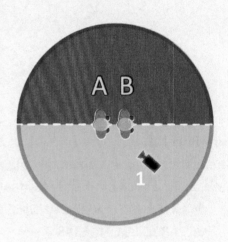

EXTERNAL REVERSE ANGLES
(Camera arrangement 1)

Camera position 2

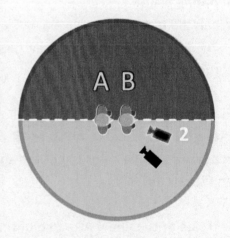

EXTERNAL REVERSE ANGLES
(Camera arrangement 1)

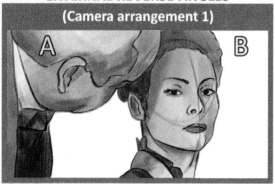

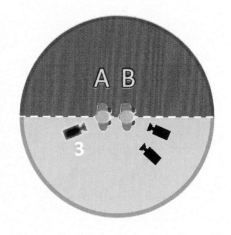

Camera position 3

PARALLEL CAMERAS
(Camera arrangement 2)

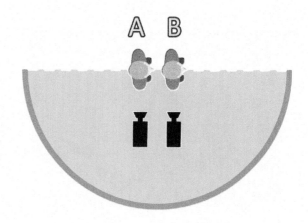

PARALLEL CAMERAS
(Camera arrangement 2)

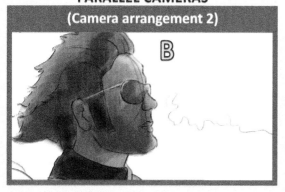

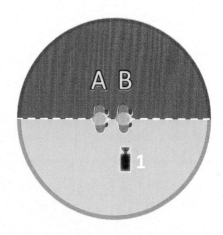

Camera position 1

PARALLEL CAMERAS
(Camera arrangement 2)

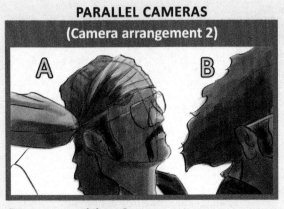
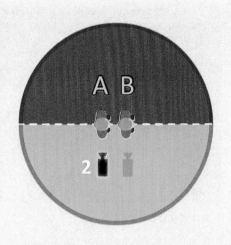

Camera position 2

PARALLEL CAMERAS
(Camera arrangement 2)

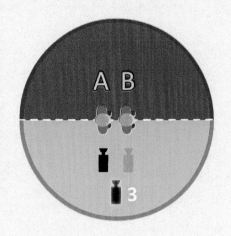

Camera position 3

5.6 • Irregular cases

Definition:

Every rule has its exceptions. An *"irregular case"* implies a variation to a basic editing or film-making principle, usually justified by a "dramatic need". Sometimes though, the need can also be due to a technical mistake of some sort, or to a lack of footage/coverage.

How it works:

There are many camera arrangements employed to cover an irregular dialogue scene between two players/actors. Let's analyse some of those which *deliberately break the 180-Degree rule.*

➔ PLAYERS HUGGING EACH OTHER
➔ CORRIDOR OR NARROW ROOM
➔ SITTING FACE TO FACE
➔ BUILDING-UP OF TENSION
➔ SITTING BACK TO BACK
➔ LYING DOWN vs SITTING

Shooting plan:

In the following examples of irregular cases the scenes start with one of the 5 basic camera arrangements we've previously spoken about. Then *the 180-Degree rule is ignored* or deliberately broken to suit a specific need. As a direct result of that, *players 'A' and 'B' exchange their positions on the screen from shot to shot.*

The reason why the 180-Degree rule was created in the first place, was not only to preserve the direction of motion inside the screen, but also to avoid getting the audience confused by a sudden change of position of one or more players within the frame at the same time. If there's not such an issue, then the rule can potentially be ignored.

In a nutshell:

Green side of the line = Regular camera arrangement. **'A'** and **'B'** keep their screen positions from shot to shot.

Red side of the line = Irregular arrangement. **'A'** and **'B'** exchange positions on the screen and the 180-Degree rule is broken.

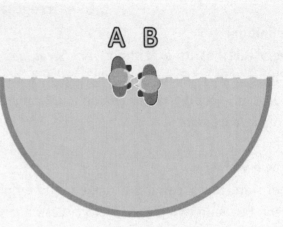

**PLAYERS HUGGING EACH OTHER
(Camera arrangement 1)**

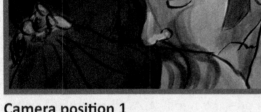

Camera position 1

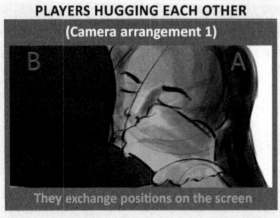

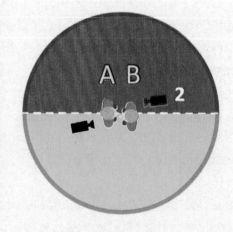

Camera position 2

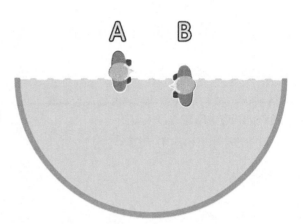

CORRIDOR OR NARROW ROOM
(Camera arrangement 2)

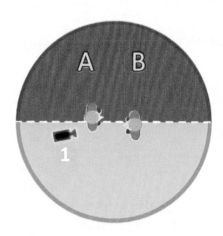

Camera position 1

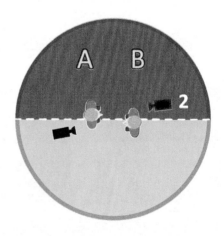

Camera position 2

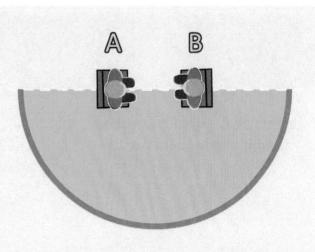

SITTING FACE TO FACE
(Camera arrangement 3)

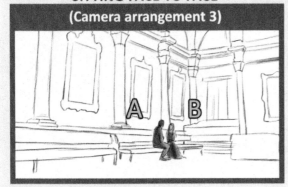

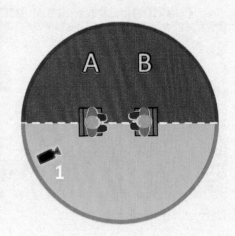

SITTING FACE TO FACE
(Camera arrangement 3)

Camera position 1

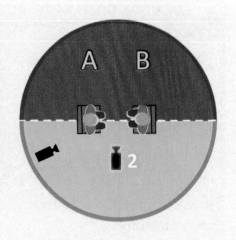

SITTING FACE TO FACE
(Camera arrangement 3)

Camera position 2

SITTING FACE TO FACE
(Camera arrangement 3)

They exchange positions on the screen

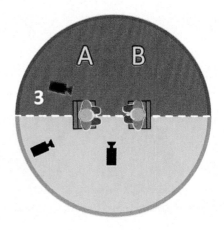

Camera position 3

SITTING FACE TO FACE
(Camera arrangement 3)

They exchange positions on the screen

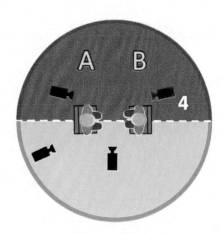

Camera position 4

BUILDING-UP OF TENSION
(Camera arrangement 4)

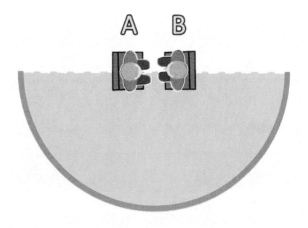

BUILDING-UP OF TENSION
(Camera arrangement 4)

Camera position 1

BUILDING-UP OF TENSION
(Camera arrangement 4)

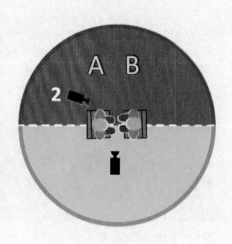 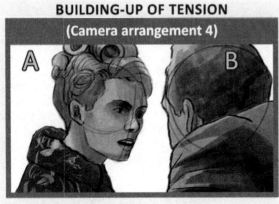

They exchange positions on the screen

Camera position 2

BUILDING-UP OF TENSION
(Camera arrangement 4)

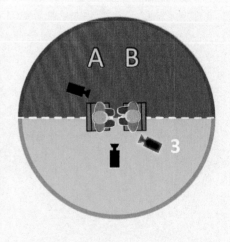

Camera position 3

SITTING BACK TO BACK
(Camera arrangement 5)

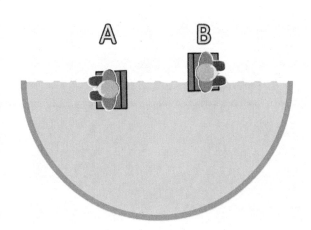

SITTING BACK TO BACK
(Camera arrangement 5)

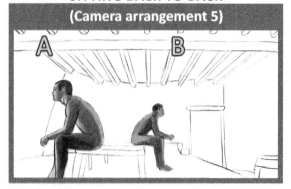

Camera position 1

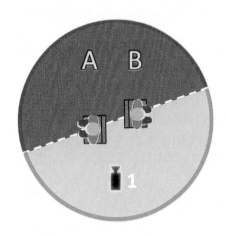

SITTING BACK TO BACK
(Camera arrangement 5)

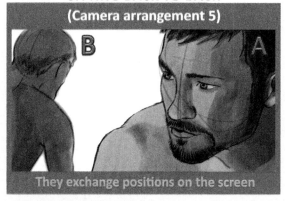

They exchange positions on the screen

Camera position 2

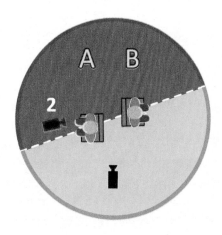

SITTING BACK TO BACK
(Camera arrangement 5)

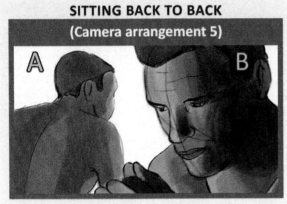

Camera position 3

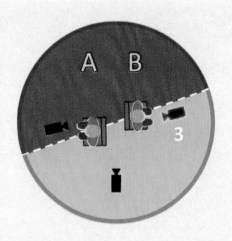

LYING DOWN vs SITTING
(Camera arrangement 6)

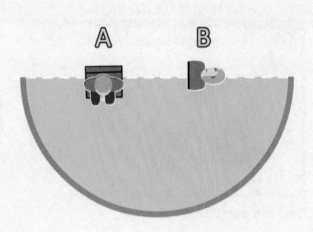

LYING DOWN vs SITTING
(Camera arrangement 6)

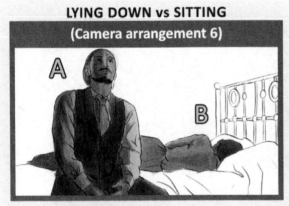

Camera position 1

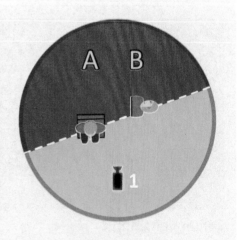

LYING DOWN vs SITTING
(Camera arrangement 6)

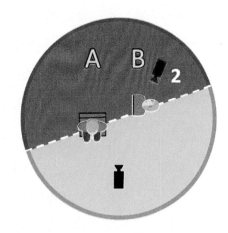

They exchange positions on the screen

Camera position 2

FAQ:

Q = Given what we've just seen, would it be correct to label an irregular case as an editing pattern which contains some sort of mistakes?

A = No, it would be incorrect. An irregular case doesn't contain any mistakes, in fact it implies an "acceptable violation" of a basic rule such as the 180-Degree rule.

Q = Why is the violation to be considered acceptable?

A = While editing, the correct players' positions on the screen is crucial to avoid a sense of confusion about "who" was "in which" place. However, sometimes dramatic and technical needs – such as a lack of coverage – take priority over basic rules (especially in static dialogue scenes where there's little or no movement at all).

PART
SIX

6

LINE OF INTEREST vs LINE OF ACTION

6.1 ● Single player

Definition:

Line of interest = Imaginary line which splits the shooting/editing space in two halves of 180 degrees each.

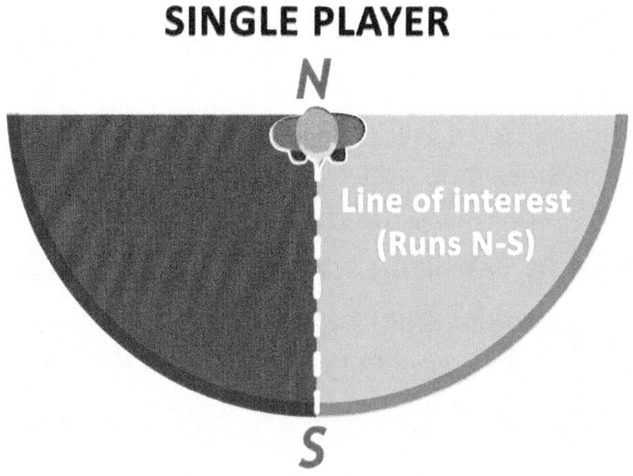

SINGLE PLAYER

N

Line of interest
(Runs N-S)

S

How it works:

When dealing with a single player the *direction in which the actor looks*, governs the line of interest.

(North-South in the previous picture. Can be East-West as well, if the actor is looking in that direction).

Line of action = It's the line which follows the *direction of motion inside the screen.* When a single player is looking North-South, the line of action usually runs East-West. That means that something relevant to the story is happening, or about to, in the East-West direction.

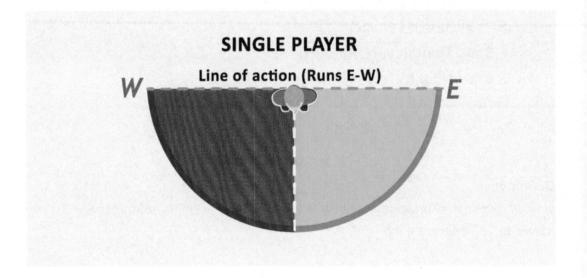

Shooting plan:

In the following example the *line of interest* runs *East-West*, between the player and the closed door, while the *line of action* runs *North-South* along the corridor, where the motion and the action occur.

Both lines intersect within the same scene, therefore when we cut from one shot to the other we break the 180-Degree rule. Yet, that is still acceptable as breaking the rule serves a specific purpose and the audience doesn't get confused about the scene's geography.

SINGLE PLAYER

Camera position 1

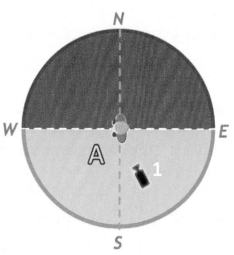

SINGLE PLAYER

Conflicting directions of movement

Camera position 2

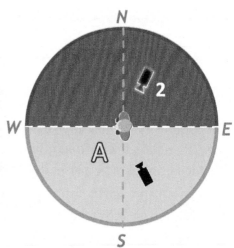

SINGLE PLAYER

Camera position 1

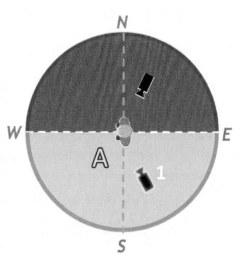

In a nutshell:

East-West = Line of interest. Always remember: when dealing with a single player *the direction in which they are looking*, sets the line.

North-South = Line of action. Cam-2 is placed in the red sector. In this specific situation that is acceptable. However we do get some conflicting directions of movement. Player **'A'** looks to screen-left in Cam position 1 and to screen-right in Cam position 2.

FAQ:

Q = The picture on page 91 shows a line of interest running North-South, while the pictures on page 93 a different one, running East-West instead. Why is it?

A = The direction in which the player is looking, sets the line of interest. It is advisable to check on a case-by-case basis in which direction the character is looking and build or edit the scene around that.

Let's keep in mind that audiences are not aware of cardinal directions, lines of interest or lines of action. These principles help the film-maker and the editor "guide" the audience through the story, avoiding confusion and letting people keep their focus on what really matters, the film. It's easy to get carried away in the editing room and waste hours trying to match "this" or "that" line with each other. Once again, pace and story first, technical nuances afterwards.

6.2 • Single vehicle

Definition:

Line of interest = Imaginary line which splits the shooting/editing space in two halves of 180 degrees each.

How it works:

With a single vehicle on the screen, the *direction in which it moves, governs the line of interest* (East-West in the following example).

Line of action = It's the line which follows the direction of motion inside the screen. With a single vehicle, *it coincides with the line of interest*, therefore it shifts along with it.

SINGLE VEHICLE

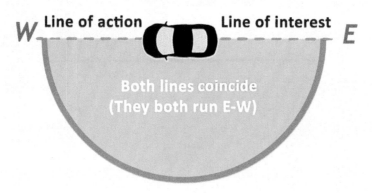

Line of action **Line of interest**

W — — — — — — — — E

**Both lines coincide
(They both run E-W)**

Shooting plan:

In the next example the *line of interest* initially runs *East-West*, because the vehicle is moving from right to left across the frame. Then, after the camera pans, we switch to a neutral direction on a North-South line.

As long as we don't cut to a shot within the vehicle, line of interest and line of action coincide and we can join the later shot with any angle available. (Which is always the case after using a neutral shot).

SINGLE VEHICLE

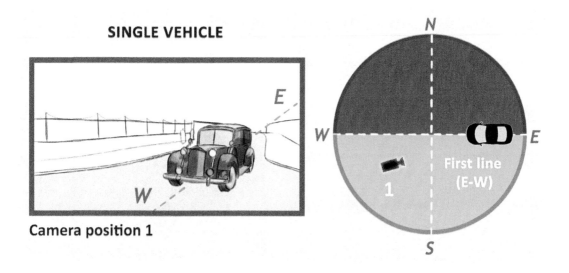

Camera position 1

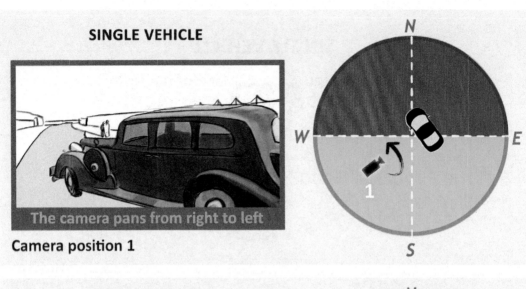

SINGLE VEHICLE

The camera pans from right to left

Camera position 1

SINGLE VEHICLE

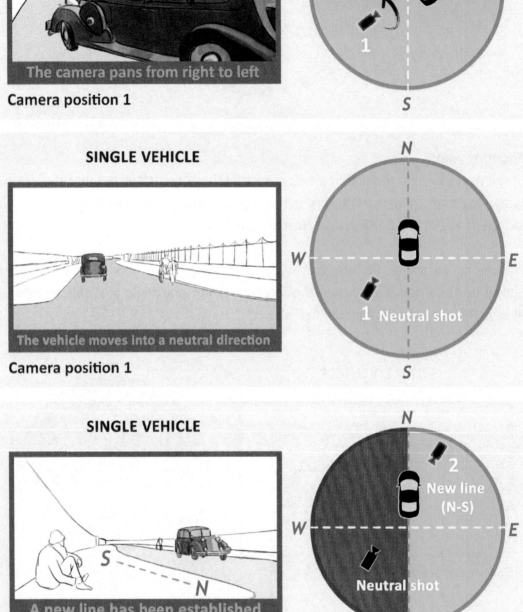

The vehicle moves into a neutral direction

Camera position 1

1 Neutral shot

SINGLE VEHICLE

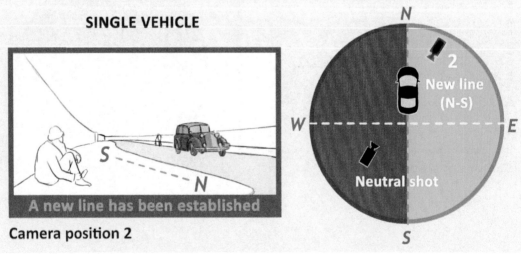

A new line has been established

Camera position 2

2 New line (N-S)

Neutral shot

As you can see from the last picture, we've established a new line, cutting to a shot placed in a sector which was previously a red one. That has been possible thanks to a neutral shot preceding cam position 2.

Once again, a neutral shot is a shot where the player or the vehicle doesn't move into a specific direction but rather away from the camera or towards it.

6.3 ● Two players + vehicle

Definition:

Line of interest = Imaginary line which splits the shooting/editing space in two halves of 180 degrees each.

How it works:

When two players are inside a moving vehicle, *the line of interest runs between their heads* (East-West in the example below).

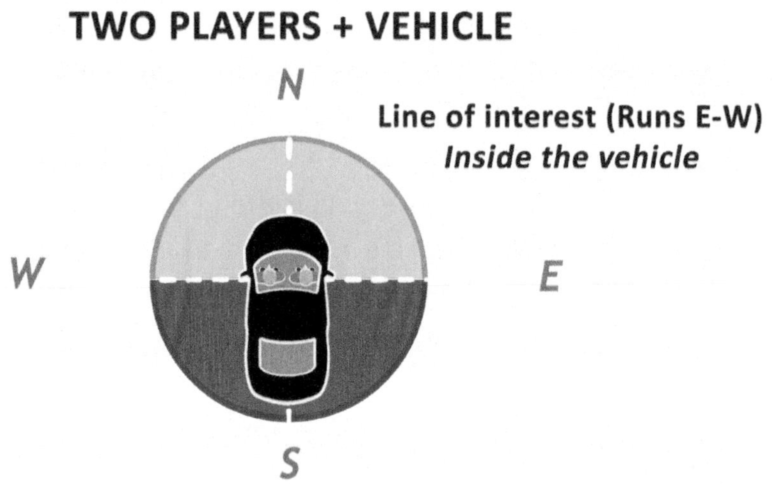

TWO PLAYERS + VEHICLE

Line of action = It's the line which follows the direction of motion inside the screen. With two players inside a vehicle, *it coincides with the direction in which the car is moving* (North-South in the following picture).

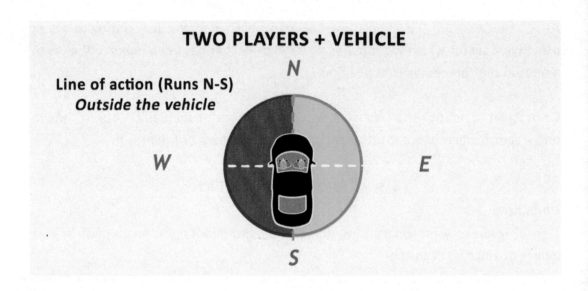

TWO PLAYERS + VEHICLE

Line of action (Runs N-S)
Outside the vehicle

Shooting plan:

In the following example, the *line of action* runs *North-South* and is established by the direction in which the vehicle is moving.

Inside the car, the *line of interest* runs *East-West.* Since the latter intersects with the former, when we cut the dialogue between the players we still follow the triangle principle applied to two actors placed side by side (See chapter 5.2).

The background behind each player is going to move into opposite directions when cutting from shot to shot. That is inevitable in a dialogue scene shot inside a moving vehicle (unless, of course, the whole scene is shot from a frontal, neutral, point of view. In that case the background will move toward a vanishing point placed behind the players).

In a nutshell:

East-West = Line of interest (players).

North-South = Line of action (vehicle).

TWO PLAYERS + VEHICLE

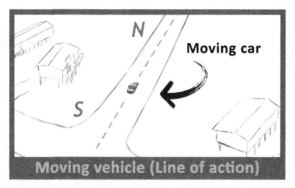

Moving car

Moving vehicle (Line of action)

Camera position 1

TWO PLAYERS + VEHICLE

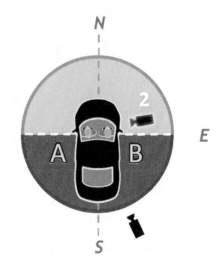

Inside the car (Line of interest)

Camera position 2

TWO PLAYERS + VEHICLE

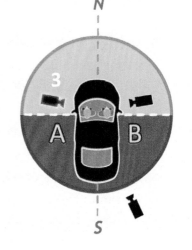

Inside the car (Line of interest)

Camera position 3

6.4 • How to "cross" the line

Definition:

Sometimes in the editing room crossing the line is inevitable. A skilled editor knows how to properly do it, switching between all the available angles without getting the audience confused and keeping the flow of the edit intact. But there are also times where a scene is intentionally shot in a way which shows on the screen a change of the line.

How it works:

Let's analyse the most popular techniques used in post production, or directly on set, to properly *cross the line.*

→ INSERT OR NEUTRAL SHOT
→ PIVOT ESTABLISHING A NEW LINE
→ PLAYER CROSSING THE LINE
→ CAMERA CROSSING THE LINE

Shooting plan:

In the following example, one side of the *line of interest* has been chosen for the main camera setup. As we can see, player **'A'** is placed on the left side of the frame while **'B'** is on the right.

If we cut to a neutral shot of either player, we can then switch to a camera angle taken from the opposite side of the line of interest. An *insert or cutaway*, would achieve of course the same result. The reason why cutaways should be used sparingly, is that they throw the audience's attention off the window if dropped into an edit without any narrative or visual connection to what's happening on the screen. I'd strongly advise not to use inserts just to fix continuity mistakes, unless the mistake itself is so big so as to get the audience confused as well. Otherwise *"the cure is worse than the disease".*

A point I won't get tired of stressing: pace and flow are going to affect the film substantially more than continuity mistakes. Some continuity issues happen so quickly on the screen that there's not even enough time to catch them. The amount of information the audience can process is limited, so let's make the most of it.

HOW TO 'CROSS' THE LINE
Insert or neutral shot (Case 1)

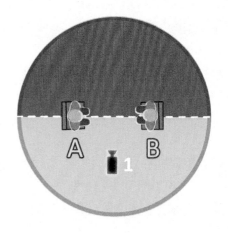

Camera position 1

HOW TO 'CROSS' THE LINE
Insert or neutral shot (Case 1)

Cut to a neutral shot

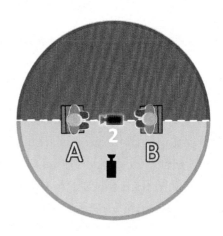

Camera position 2

HOW TO 'CROSS' THE LINE
Insert or neutral shot (Case 1)

Crossing to the other side of the line

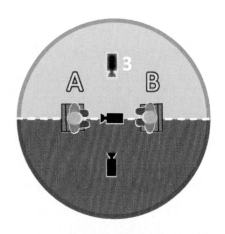

Camera position 3

Both players switched sides, with **'B'** ending up on the left and **'A'** on the right. That is precisely the goal the film-makers were trying to achieve. Whether a deliberate shooting decision or a post production necessity, the use of a neutral shot helped them to establish a brand new line of interest. Hopefully the audience didn't get confused too much by the change in the background (From the restaurant window to the main dining room).

Shooting plan:
In the next example, one side of the *line of interest* has been chosen for the main camera setup. As we can see, player **'A'** is placed on the left side of the frame, **'B'** is in the middle and **'C'** on the right. They're walking towards the camera when a fourth player, **'D'**, steps into the frame from behind them, in the background of the shot.

'B', the dominant player, is used as a *pivot to achieve a change in the line of interest.* As soon as he turns back to face **'D'**, a new line, running North-South between them, is established.

At this stage, the editor is free to stick with the new line and use any available angles which work accordingly with it. Technically speaking things are a bit more complicated than this. Potentially we can still jump back on the old line if the pivot turns once again to face **'A'** or **'C'**, but for the sake of simplicity we'll skip that eventuality for now.

This type of situation is extremely common when dealing with dialogue scenes involving three or more actors on the screen at the same time. There's also the chance that the coverage of the scene was so huge that multiple angles taken from different sides of the same line of interest, or even from multiple lines at the same time, ended up being shot on set. There is no one size fits all unfortunately, that's why grasping the basics will allow editors and film-makers to work on a case-by-case basis and make the decision that makes more sense, based on time/budget constraints on set, or footage availability in the editing room. Never complain about "that" missing shot or camera angle. The craft is not into cutting the best scene with the highest number of options available, but making the most out of what's actually being shot.

HOW TO 'CROSS' THE LINE

Pivot establishing a new line (Case 2)

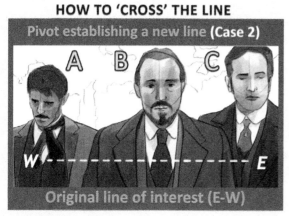

Original line of interest (E-W)

Camera position 1

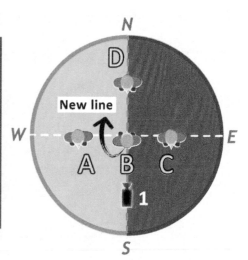

HOW TO 'CROSS' THE LINE

Pivot establishing a new line (Case 2)

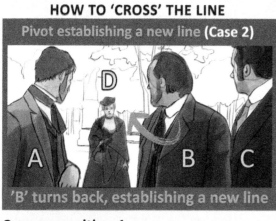

'B' turns back, establishing a new line

Camera position 1

HOW TO 'CROSS' THE LINE

Pivot establishing a new line (Case 2)

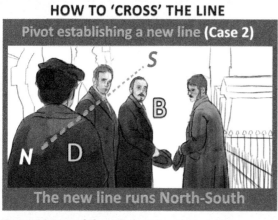

The new line runs North-South

Camera position 2

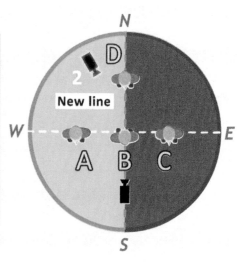

Shooting plan:

In the third example, one side of the *line of interest* has been chosen for the main camera setup, a pair of external/internal reverse angles. As we can see, player **'A'** is placed on the left side of the frame, **'B'** is on the right.

Since static dialogue scenes can be pretty boring[3], at some point we see **'A'** standing up from where he's sitting and completely cross the line of interest to land on a couch across from him. While he's doing so the camera pans along with him from left to right. **'B'** doesn't move at all, keeping the same position he originally had within the frame.

Once the new position of player 'A' is achieved, the old line of interest is replaced with a new one, making the previous internal reverse angle on him (Cam-1) impossible to use once again, as it would break the 180-Degree rule. We need to cut to angles taken from the new side of the line of interest. Player **'A'**, who was previously placed on the left side of the screen, is now placed on the right, achieving a different shot composition.

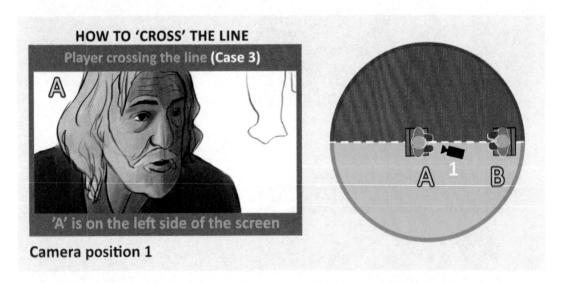

HOW TO 'CROSS' THE LINE
Player crossing the line (Case 3)
'A' is on the left side of the screen

Camera position 1

---

3 Camera movements and changes in the blocking of the scene usually add variety to an otherwise iterative and boring editing pattern.

HOW TO 'CROSS' THE LINE

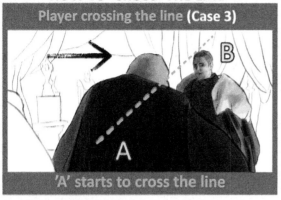

Camera position 2

HOW TO 'CROSS' THE LINE

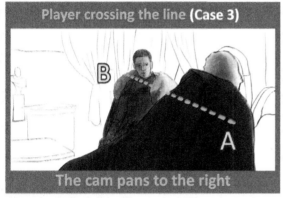

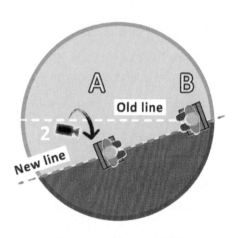

Camera position 2

HOW TO 'CROSS' THE LINE

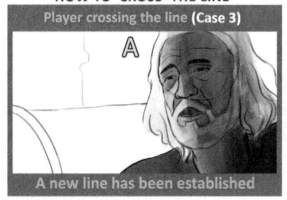

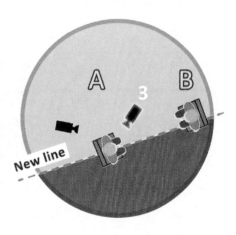

Camera position 3

Shooting plan:

In the final example, one side of the *line of interest* has been chosen for the main camera setup, which is a pair of external reverse angles. As we can see, player **'A'** is placed on the left side of the frame, **'B'** in the middle and **'C'** on the right. Since **'B'** is a passive player and the attention is focused only on **'A'** and **'C'**, for the sake of this example we'll ignore him completely.

The camera slides laterally from behind the back of **'C'**, crossing the initial line and creating a new one on the opposite side of the player. As a result of the new line of interest running between the characters, **'A'** and **'C'** who were placed originally on the left and right sides of the screen, now switch positions. That is precisely what is supposed to happen.

Through a camera movement the change of line is shown directly on the screen, within the frame, and the audience witnesses it. This trick helps the viewer get a sense of the scene geography keeping track of the characters' positions, without being distracted by an otherwise abrupt cut from the green to the red side of the line of interest.

The new line will consistently keep the players on the new sides of the screen, no matter how many times we cut from an external reverse of **'A'** to one of **'C'**.

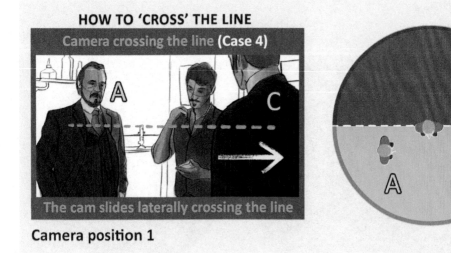

Camera position 1

HOW TO 'CROSS' THE LINE

Camera crossing the line (Case 4)

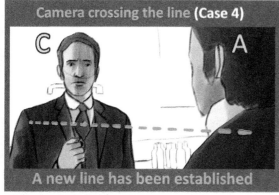

'A' and 'C' switch screen sides

Camera position 2

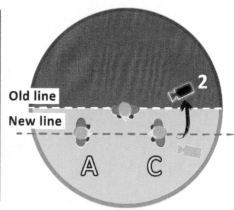

Old line

New line

HOW TO 'CROSS' THE LINE

Camera crossing the line (Case 4)

A new line has been established

Camera position 3

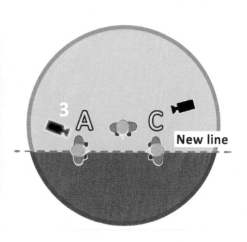

New line

Even though the camera movement clearly gives away the presence of the shooting equipment on set[4] – potentially diverting people's attention – it still achieves the desired effect of crossing the line, which eventually improves the viewers' watching experience (avoiding confusion about the characters' positions on the screen).

---

4 This is especially true when there's little or no action/movement on the screen.

PART
SEVEN

7

DIALOGUE: THREE PLAYERS/ACTORS

7.1 ● Straight line

7.2 ● Right angle

7.3 ● Triangle formation

7.4 ● Number contrast

7.5 ● Pivoting

A three-player dialogue scene is a type of scene where three actors are present on screen at the same time. There have been *many different approaches* developed over the years to cover and edit this type of scene. Let's start with some basic concepts.

The *line of interest* running between the players is based on the camera arrangement chosen to cover the scene.

In a *regular case*, the characters keep the same screen positions while cutting between shots. If they exchange positions, the case is deemed *irregular.*

In the event of an irregular case, there are several principles to keep in mind in order to keep visual consistency on the screen and let the audience enjoy the film without getting confused by the characters' positioning. But let's proceed step by step as things are going to get slightly more complicated from now on. We're still talking about basic principles, but the higher the number of players on the screen the higher the number of variables to keep under control.

THREE-PLAYER DIALOGUE

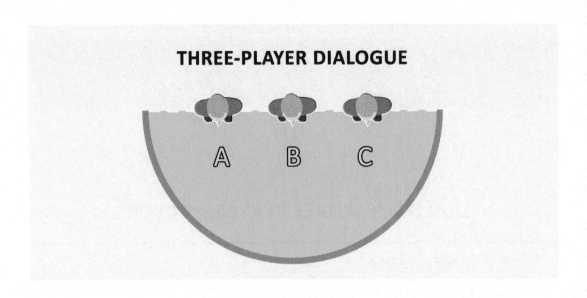

7.1 • Straight line

Definition:

The *most basic camera arrangement* used to shoot a three-player dialogue. It's covered with two external reverse cam positions.

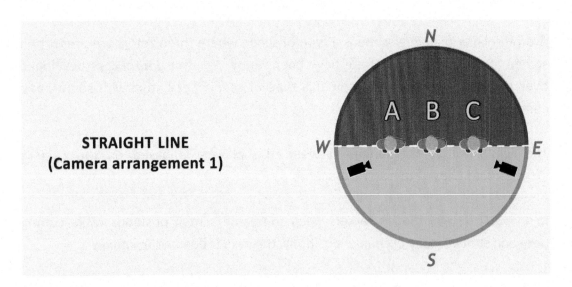

STRAIGHT LINE
(Camera arrangement 1)

How it works:

All the *players are in a straight line* and keep their screen area from shot to shot. Usually they all stand close to each other. Further variations are also possible though, including one or two seated next to a central performer.

Shooting plan:

Regardless of the players standing or sitting, this kind of approach may lead to *iterative editing patterns*: 1-2-1-2. As we'll see in the following examples, the characters stay in their screen area from master shot to master shot.

Often the player in the centre of the frame is the leading one. The attention is focused on him, but it's not unlikely to use player **'B'** merely as a pivot to switch the attention from **'A'** to **'C'.** That is of course something related to the story we're trying to tell, therefore to the point of view from which the audience "witnesses" what's happening on the screen. It is not something we should be adamant about. One or multiple pivots have to serve the purpose of helping the film-maker move the story forward.

Another tiny caveat. In the following examples, external camera angles are employed to cover the whole dialogue. We switch from master to master without singling out one or more characters at the same time. That leads the focus on the actors' performances, as the viewers' attention will be mainly redirected by their words, rather than by a specific camera angle. It's way easier to make the audience focus on a close up shot of a character, rather than a wide angle of a group of them.

In a nutshell:

Green side of the line = Regular case: the players keep the *same screen positions* from shot to shot.

Red side of the line = No cam positions employed. We won't be able to cut to a shot taken from the red side of the line of interest.

STRAIGHT LINE

Standing players (Cam arrangement 1)

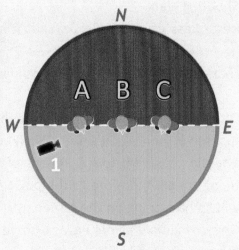

Camera position 1

STRAIGHT LINE

Standing players (Cam arrangement 1)

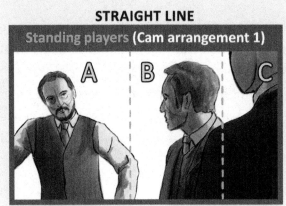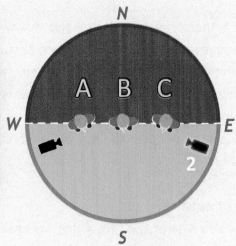

Camera position 2

STRAIGHT LINE

Standing players (Cam arrangement 1)

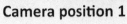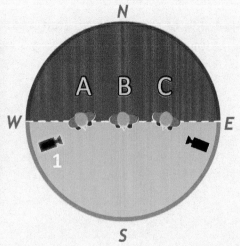

Camera position 1

STRAIGHT LINE

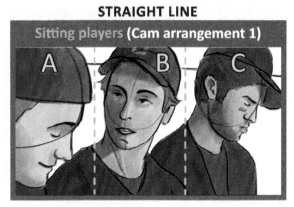

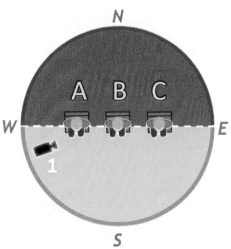

Camera position 1

STRAIGHT LINE

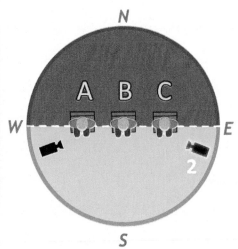

Camera position 2

STRAIGHT LINE

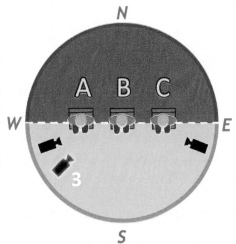

Camera position 3

7.2 • Right angle

Definition:

A second *basic arrangement* used to shoot a three-player dialogue. It's covered with *external right angle cam* positions.

How it works:

The *players are in a right angle position* ("L" shape) and keep their screen area from shot to shot. Usually when they sit together, one is dominant over the other two. However, it is also possible to come across cases where all the players are standing.

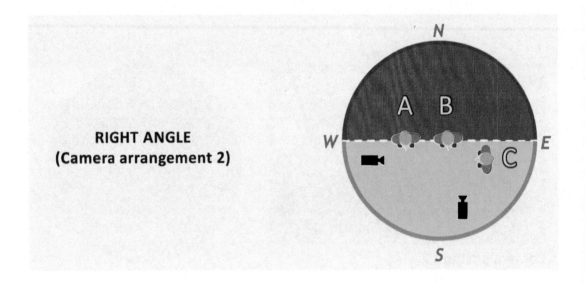

RIGHT ANGLE
(Camera arrangement 2)

Shooting plan:

The same rules outlined when the players are in a straight line, apply to the right angle arrangement as well. If the footage allows a degree of variety in terms of available shot sizes, it's strongly advisable to exploit it, in order to avoid iterative editing patterns. Making use of closer or wider angles is an easy solution to add variety to an otherwise pretty standard pattern. But once again, let's always keep in mind that highly effective dialogue scenes are successful in moving the story forward. It's great to add variety to an editing pattern but without losing sight of what counts the most.

RIGHT ANGLE

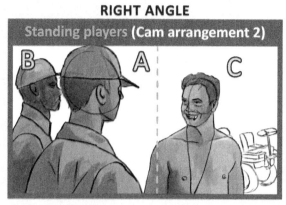

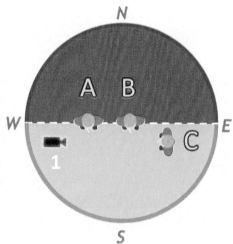

Camera position 1

RIGHT ANGLE

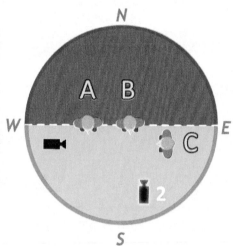

Camera position 2

RIGHT ANGLE

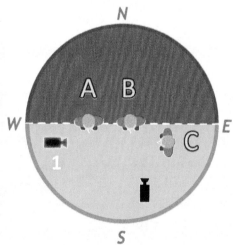

Camera position 1

117

RIGHT ANGLE

Sitting players (Cam arrangement 2)

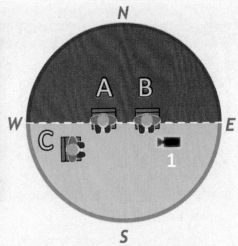

Camera position 1

RIGHT ANGLE

Sitting players (Cam arrangement 2)

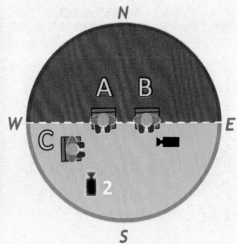

Camera position 2

RIGHT ANGLE

Sitting players (Cam arrangement 2)

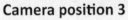
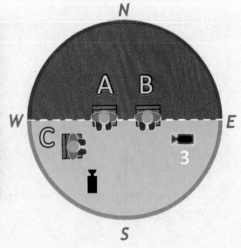

Camera position 3

7.3 • Triangle formation

Three players involved in a dialogue scene, are often arranged in a triangle formation. There have been several approaches developed over the years to cover and edit this type of scene.

We will focus on *three formulas* which use *only external reverse cam positions.* External reverse cam positions applied to a three-player triangle arrangement, always make this approach an *irregular case*. The characters never stay in a steady screen area from shot to shot and constantly switch positions. Let's see why.

TRIANGLE FORMATION

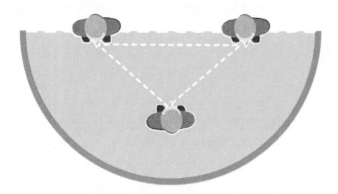

Definition:
To cover this type of dialogue scene you can choose two sets of cameras at the same time (see next picture).
Based on the cam positions chosen, the result will be one of *three different editing patterns.* It takes time to get familiar with all these formulas, but once you grasp the basics, things will become much easier to handle on set and in post.

Triangle formations have many "composition" advantages. By placing the characters in such a shape we can visually achieve different moods and vibes, delivering different emotions and feelings. Just think about the way a triangle recedes into the horizon can create the impression of perspective and depth.

Or perhaps of the way a player placed at the vertex of a triangle formation is perceived by the audience. Is the character powerful, dominant, leader of a group? Triangles also combine with backgrounds and architectural structures placed within the frame: a playground for DOPs and directors.

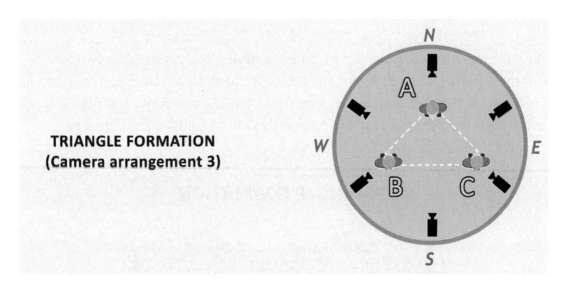

TRIANGLE FORMATION
(Camera arrangement 3)

How it works:
The players are in a triangle formation and *change their screen area* from shot to shot (all of them, apart from the *dominant player*).
Usually they all stand close to each other. However, there are many more possible variations, such as lying down, seating or a mix of both.

Let's finally have a look at the *three editing patterns.*

➔ CENTRAL DOMINANT PLAYER
- The dominant player, '**A**', stays in the same screen area from shot to shot. '**B**' and '**C**' exchange positions.

➔ NO DOMINANT PLAYER
- None of the players stay in the same screen area from shot to shot. However, '**A**' and '**B**' keep their *relative screen positions.*

➔ LATERAL DOMINANT PLAYER
- The dominant player, '**B**', keeps a lateral screen area from shot to shot. '**A**' and '**C**' exchange positions.

Shooting plan:

It's crucial to clarify that when we talk about *"dominant player"*, it means that one of the characters involved in a three-player dialogue scene, and in a triangle formation in particular, *always keeps the same screen area from shot to shot.*

Relative screen positions = Here's where things start to get a bit more complicated. When two players keep their "relative" screen positions on the screen it means that even though they move from one side to the other of the screen as a result of the editing pattern chosen, *they don't switch positions relative to each other, but on the screen only.*

TRIANGLE FORMATION

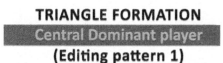

(Editing pattern 1)

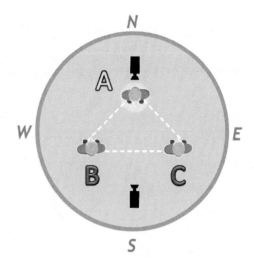

TRIANGLE FORMATION

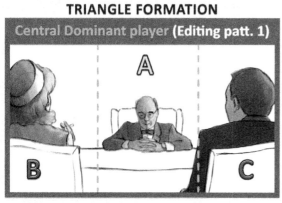

Camera position 1

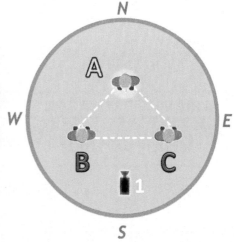

TRIANGLE FORMATION

Central Dominant player (Editing patt. 1)

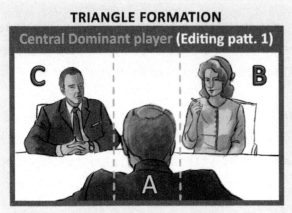

Camera position 2

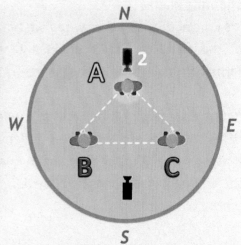

TRIANGLE FORMATION

Central Dominant player (Editing patt. 1)

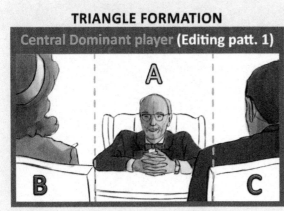

Camera position 1

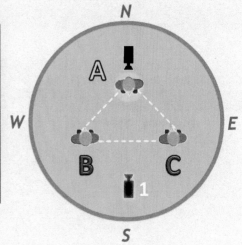

TRIANGLE FORMATION

No Dominant player
(Editing pattern 2)

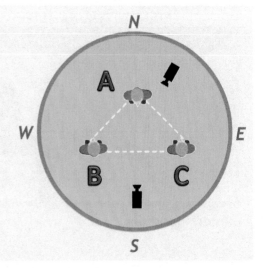

TRIANGLE FORMATION
No Dominant player (Editing patt. 2)

Same relative positions: B-A

Camera position 1

TRIANGLE FORMATION
No Dominant player (Editing patt. 2)

Same relative positions: B-A

Camera position 2

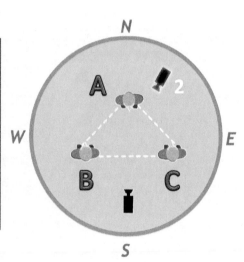

TRIANGLE FORMATION
No Dominant player (Editing patt. 2)

Same relative positions: B-A

Camera position 1

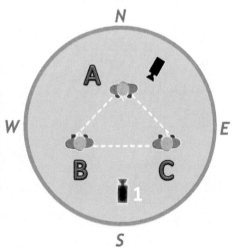

TRIANGLE FORMATION
Lateral Dominant player
(Editing pattern 3)

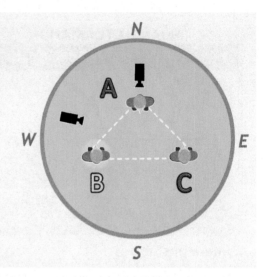

TRIANGLE FORMATION
Lateral Dominant player (Editing patt. 3)

Camera position 1

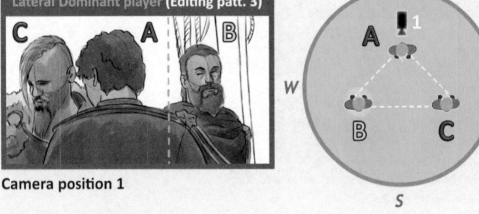

TRIANGLE FORMATION
Lateral Dominant player (Editing patt. 3)

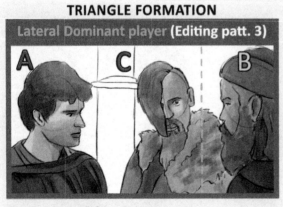

Camera position 2

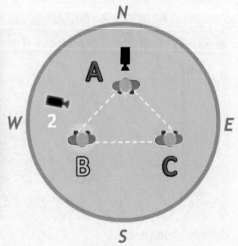

124

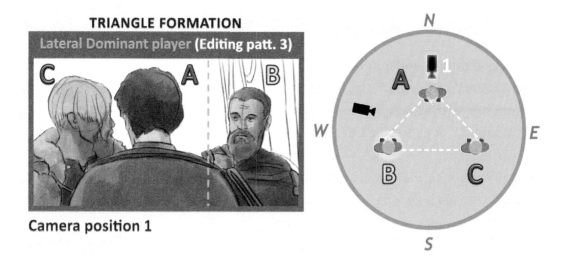

Camera position 1

In a nutshell:
Yellow letter = The player always keeps the same screen area from shot to shot (dominant).

Red letter = The player changes screen area from shot to shot.

FAQ:
Q = Why is a player considered as a dominant one, even though they don't necessarily "dominate" the scene being the real centre of attention?
A = *A player can be dominant in several ways* and the concept itself shouldn't be misunderstood. When we edit a dialogue scene with three players involved, arranged in a triangle formation, in two cases out of three one player "dominates" a screen area from shot to shot. It doesn't necessarily mean that they are also the leading player.

Q = What's the difference between dominant player and leading player?
A = The *dominant player* keeps the same screen area from shot to shot. *The leading player is usually the one who's predominant from the narrative point of view.* All the attention is on them even when changing screen area from shot to shot.

7.4 ● Number contrast

Definition:
Opposing external and internal reverse camera arrangements provide what is called *"Number contrast"*. The number of players on screen changes from shot to shot: from a take including three players (**'A'**, **'B'** and **'C'**) to a different one keeping only **'B'** and **'C'**, or even **'C'** alone, on the screen.

Generally the external camera positions cover the whole group of players, while the internal ones only a part of it. This approach adds visual variety to a triangular formation of players.

How it works:
Let's analyse several *cases of number contrast.*
- → EXTERNAL/INTERNAL CAMS – 3 to 1
- → EXTERNAL/INTERNAL CAMS – 3 to 2
- → INTERNAL CAMS – 2 to 1
- → PARALLEL CAMS – 3 to 2 – 2 to 1
- → COMMON VISUAL AXIS – 3 to 1

Shooting plan:
There can be different reasons for adding number contrast to a dialogue scene. Often this kind of technique helps the editor to focus on a single player or a small group of them.

In a nutshell:
Through a mix of the *5 basic camera arrangements* (see chapter 4.3) the editor can isolate one or more players from the rest of the triangle formation.

Let's always keep in mind that great storytelling comes from the perfect mixture of the film-making elements: dialogue, camera angle, cinematography, editing. The main goal is to keep the audience hooked, completely absorbed by the narrative. If we feel that three players on the screen at the same time are too many and the need arises to focus only on one of them, it's time to use all the tricks available to lead the viewers into the direction we want them to go. Make them laugh, make them cry, but no matter what keep them engaged.

NUMBER CONTRAST
External/Internal cams - 3 to 1
(Case 1)

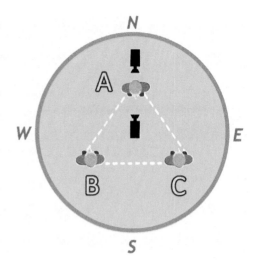

NUMBER CONTRAST
External/Internal cams - 3 to 1 (Case 1)

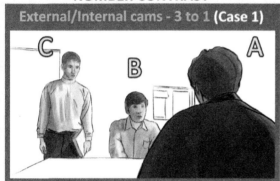

Camera position 1

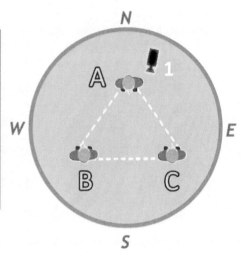

NUMBER CONTRAST
External/Internal cams - 3 to 1 (Case 1)

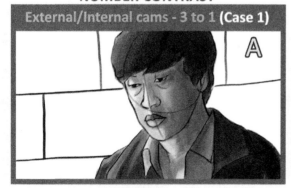

Camera position 2

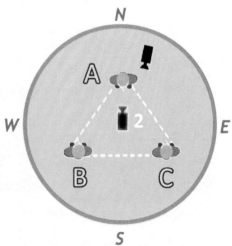

NUMBER CONTRAST
External/Internal cams - 3 to 2
(Case 2)

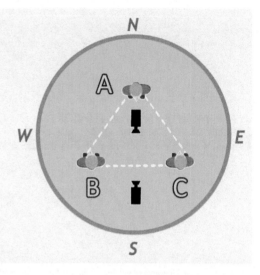

NUMBER CONTRAST
External/Internal cams - 3 to 2 (Case 2)

Camera position 1

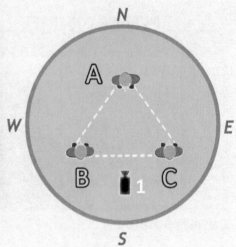

NUMBER CONTRAST
External/Internal cams - 3 to 2 (Case 2)

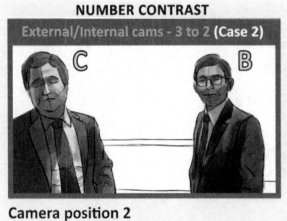

Camera position 2

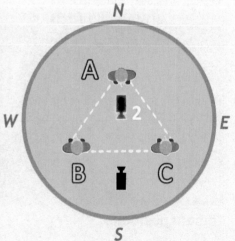

NUMBER CONTRAST
Internal cams - 2 to 1
(Case 3)

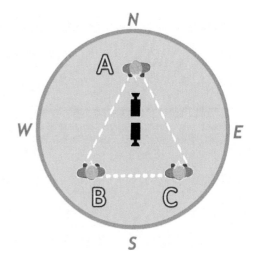

NUMBER CONTRAST
Internal cams - 2 to 1 **(Case 3)**

Camera position 1

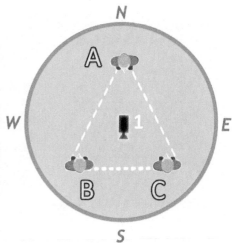

NUMBER CONTRAST
Internal cams - 2 to 1 **(Case 3)**

Camera position 2

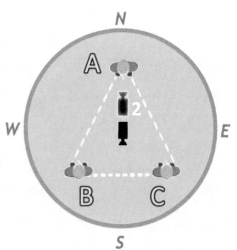

NUMBER CONTRAST
Parallel cams - 3 to 2 - 2 to 1
(Case 4)

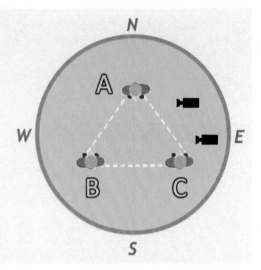

NUMBER CONTRAST
Parallel cams - 3 to 2 - 2 to 1 (Case 4)

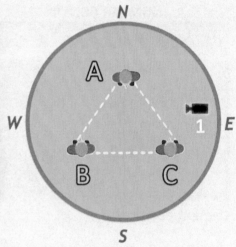

Camera position 1

NUMBER CONTRAST
Parallel cams - 3 to 2 - 2 to 1 (Case 4)

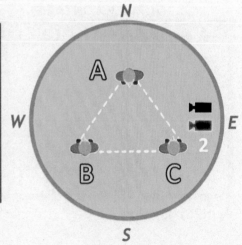

Camera position 2

NUMBER CONTRAST

Parallel cams - 3 to 2 - 2 to 1 (Case 4)

Camera position 3

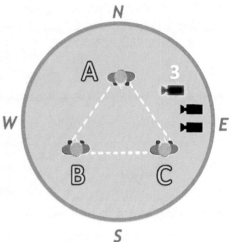

NUMBER CONTRAST

Common visual axis - 3 to 1 (Case 5)

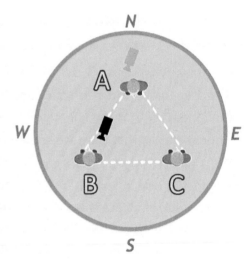

NUMBER CONTRAST

Common visual axis - 3 to 1 (Case 5)

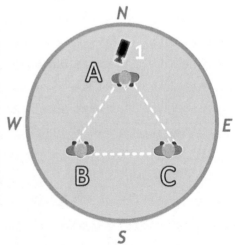

Camera position 1

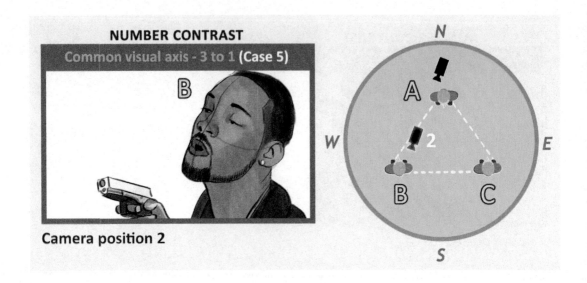

Camera position 2

7.5 • Pivoting

Definition:

Sometimes when editors cut a dialogue scene between three players, it might be necessary, for narrative or pacing reasons, to focus only on two of them at the same time. If one of the characters becomes the point of reference for the change of shot, it means that they are used as a *"pivot"*.

Through the use of pivots we can help the audiences "find their way around", keeping track of where the players moved within the frame.

There are several different approaches to this technique, as the pivot can assume different positions on the screen. Most of the time *pivoting works well* when dealing *with triangular or linear formations.*

How it works:

Let's finally have a look at four *pivoting patterns.*

→ PIVOT SAME SIDE

- Player **'A'**, is used as a "fixed" pivot to shoot (or to cut to) a pair of external cam positions of **'B'** and **'C'**.

→ PIVOT SHIFTS SIDES

- Player **'A'**, is used as a "shifting" pivot to shoot (or to cut to) a pair of external reverse cam positions of **'B'** and **'C'**.

➜ PIVOT BACKGROUND/FOREGROUND
- Player **'A'**, is used as a fixed pivot to shoot (or to cut to) a pair of external reverse cam positions of **'B'** and **'C'**.

➜ PIVOT CHANGE OF LINE
- Player **'A'** *(pivot)*, and **cam 1** *(bridge shot)* are both used as pivots to shoot (or to cut to) a pair of external cam positions of **'B'** and **'C'**.

Pivoting can be applied to a three-player dialogue scene regardless of the characters' body positions. Triangular formations, right angles, linear dispositions, they are all suitable to make use of this technique. *You can use either a cam* position *or a player, to create a pivot.*

Usually a camera position used as a pivot is called a *bridge shot.* Basically it is a type of shot which links/connects two players, or camera positions, which wouldn't work from a continuity point of view if cut back-to-back, one after the other. We need a "bridge" between them in order to preserve visual consistency and flow.

Shooting plan:
In the following example (PIVOT SAME SIDE) player **'A'** (fixed pivot) always keeps the same screen area. His position is used to cut to either **'B'** *or* **'C'**.

PIVOTING
Pivot same side
(Editing patt. 1)

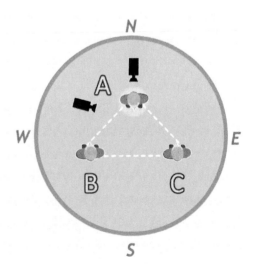

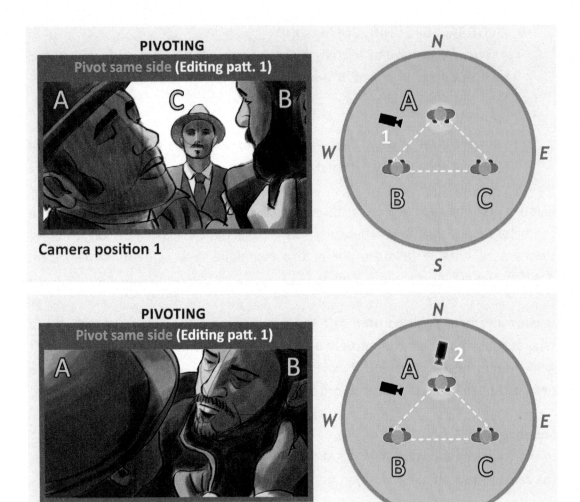

PIVOTING

Pivot same side (Editing patt. 1)

Camera position 1

PIVOTING

Pivot same side (Editing patt. 1)

Camera position 2

Shooting plan:

In the next example (PIVOT SHIFTS SIDE), player **'A'** *(shifting pivot)* changes screen area from shot to shot while cutting to reverse cam positions of **'B'** and **'C'**.

This is often the case when a player is leaning against a wall or an object, shifting gaze between two other players placed at the opposite sides of a room (sitting or standing across from each other while the pivot is located in the middle). Even though we actually have a stationary pivot within the frame, the character nevertheless *"shifts"* from one side to the other of the screen, namely from left to right and the other way around.

PIVOTING
Pivot shifts sides
(Editing patt. 2)

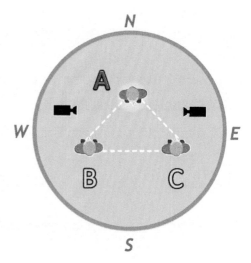

PIVOTING
Pivot shifts sides (Editing patt. 2)

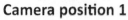

Camera position 1

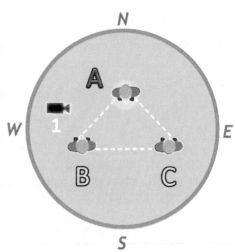

PIVOTING
Pivot shifts sides (Editing patt. 2)

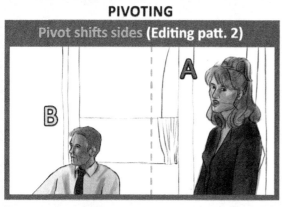

Camera position 2

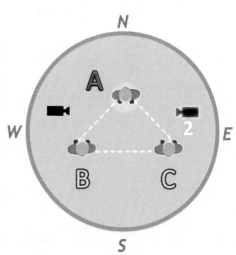

Shooting plan:

Next one (PIVOT BACKGROUND/FOREGROUND). Player **'A'** *(fixed pivot)* "moves"[5] from the background in cam-1, to the foreground in cam-2. While we alternate cam-1 and 2, we can also cover players **'B'** and **'C'**. It's important to underline the fact that player **'A'** always keeps the same screen area from shot to shot.

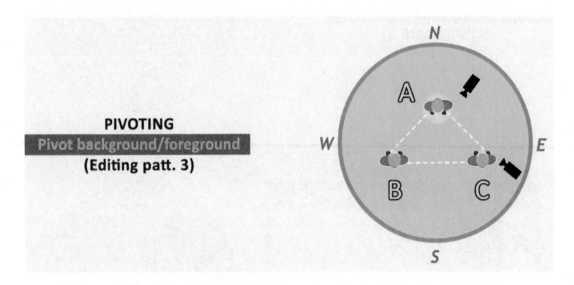

PIVOTING

Pivot background/foreground

(Editing patt. 3)

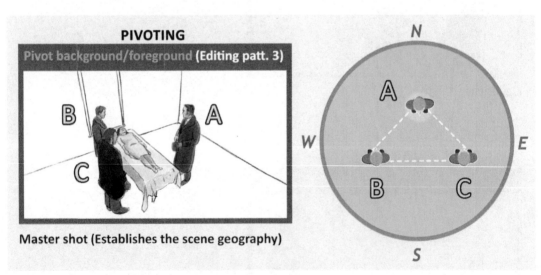

PIVOTING

Pivot background/foreground **(Editing patt. 3)**

Master shot (Establishes the scene geography)

---

5 By saying that the player "moves", we merely mean it from the standpoint of the shot composition. The actor himself doesn't physically move within the frame. He keeps standing still throughout the whole scene. Therefore, we still refer to him as a "fixed" pivot.

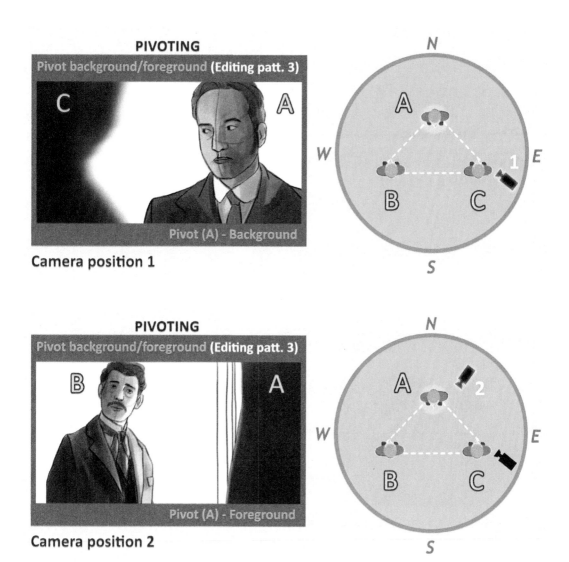

Camera position 1

Camera position 2

Shooting plan:

In the final example (PIVOT CHANGE OF LINE), we have *two pivots*: *Player A* (pivot) and *Cam 1* (pivot/bridge shot). When '**A**' looks at '**C**' or '**B**', cam-1 is used as a bridge to achieve a smooth change of line from **A-C** to **A-B**.

This is a must-know rule editors should always be aware of when dealing with a change of line on screen. Keeping screen directions clear helps avoid making the audience feel confused, therefore losing interest in what's happening within the frame.

PIVOTING
Pivot change of line
(Editing patt. 4)

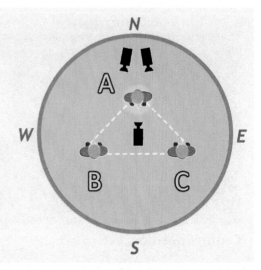

PIVOTING
Pivot change of line (Editing patt. 4)

Master shot (Establishes the scene geography)

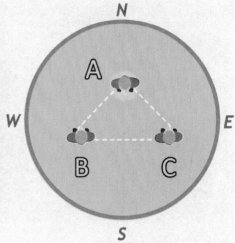

PIVOTING
Pivot change of line (Editing patt. 4)

Pivot (A) - Bridge shot (cam-1)

Camera position 1

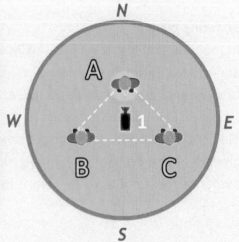

PIVOTING

Pivot change of line (Editing patt. 4)

Camera position 2

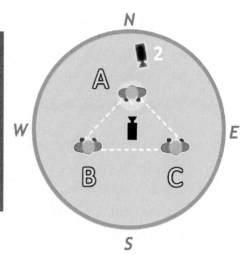

PIVOTING

Pivot change of line (Editing patt. 4)

Pivot (A) - Bridge shot (cam-1)

Camera position 1

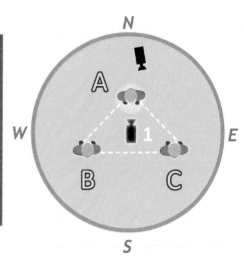

PIVOTING

Pivot change of line (Editing patt. 4)

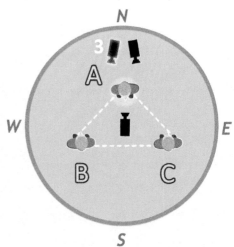

Camera position 3

These types of film-making tricks and nuances are actually what makes some films feel flawless to the audience. There is a clear visual connection between shots, a steady pace they can follow and an overall fluidity to the whole piece that makes the cuts go unnoticed, which is the ultimate goal of great editing. *Sad but true about editing: It's there only to go unnoticed.*

I truly believe that comparing editing with traditional grammar and punctuation is not a far fetched idea. Punctuation separates sentences (rather than shots) and clarifies how a sentence should be read, influencing the meaning or reception of written communication. Editing does precisely the same, making scenes or sequences more clear to the audience.

PART
EIGHT

8

CUT ON ACTION vs CUT AFTER THE MOVEMENT

Not all the cuts are born equal. This might sound like a cliché but it is in my opinion one of the basic foundations upon which editing and film-making have been thriving on, over the past century. If it was only a matter of switching between camera angles in a dialogue scene, cinema would be long dead now. Yes, you should grasp the basics and know the rules. And yes, from time to time if there's a narrative purpose to serve you should also break them and see what fits best for the film.

But ultimately what really makes the difference between a story people are drawn into and one which they just passively witness sipping fizzy drinks on the couch, is the depth of the craftsmanship behind the production. *"Where", "when" and "how" to make a cut* are extremely serious topics you should never gloss over.

The combination and chemistry between all these elements gives life to that wonderful magic we call cinema. That absorbing and satisfying experience audiences are willing to pay for. Through our technical knowledge we can transport people from their everyday life to a world of wonders which makes them forget their struggles and problems. In that, I truly believe film-making is a therapeutic craft.

8.1 • Cut on action

Definition:

Cut on action = It's the most extensively used technique for continuity editing. The movement of the player on the screen, begins in the first shot and finishes in the second.

How it works:

A good cut on action should seamlessly join two or more shots, interrupting and restarting the movement shown on the screen multiple times, always avoiding abrupt jumps. One of the most popular principles to properly perform a cut on action is the *"One-third/Two-thirds principle"*.

Editor's timeline:

In the following example we've got a samurai fighting scene. Player **'A'** *begins* a movement in *Shot 1* and *ends* it in *Shot 2.* Through these two cuts the editor seamlessly shows a complete movement on the screen. It goes without saying that the fighting carries on for a while. Within this sequence there's a variety of interconnected cuts on action, in a pleasing flow of movement which keeps the viewer engaged and absorbed by the action. If you don't "see" the cut, you don't "feel" it. Funnily enough this basic principle leads to a very controversial topic in the editing world: "When/Where" to apply a cut.

CUT ON ACTION

Shot 1 = The movement begins here   Shot 2 = The movement ends here

8.2 • The one-third-/two-thirds principle

Definition:

One-third/Two-thirds principle = Basic editing principle which helps the editor achieve a smooth, seamless cut on action between two shots. Timing is the key factor this principle is based upon.

How it works:

As a rule of thumb, when the editor cuts on action, every time that a new movement begins on the screen, it should be shown for *one-third* of its overall length in the first shot and for the *remaining two-thirds* in the following one. It works the other way around too.

ONE-THIRD/TWO-THIRDS PRINCIPLE

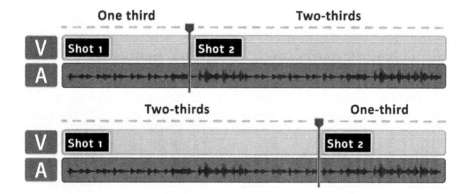

Editor's timeline:

First example (1/3 – 2/3) = In shot 1, the player starts to turn his body from left to right. After about 1/3 of the movement, cut to shot 2, where the remaining 2/3 is completed.

ONE-THIRD/TWO-THIRDS PRINCIPLE

Shot 1 = The movement begins here   **Shot 2 = The movement ends here**

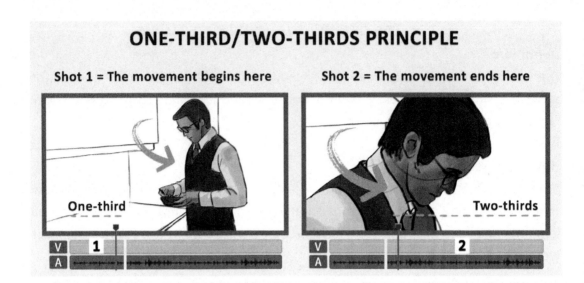

Second example (2/3 – 1/3) **=** In shot 1, the player starts to turn his head from left to right. After about 2/3 of the movement, cut to shot 2, where the remaining 1/3 is completed.

ONE-THIRD/TWO-THIRDS PRINCIPLE

Shot 1 = The movement begins here   **Shot 2 = The movement ends here**

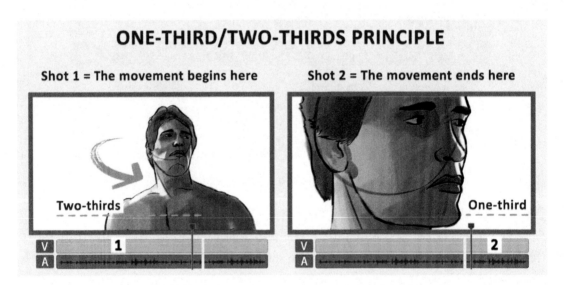

Please never forget that the rule we just outlined is a general principle which might not work all the time and in all the different circumstances. A good cut most often "feels" good. Feel free to disregard this principle if it doesn't fit your specific edit. Nothing is set in stone when it comes to achieving smooth cuts.

8.3 • Cut after the movement

Definition:

Cut after movement = The player on screen completes a movement in the first shot, then the editor cuts to the second one. This type of technique is often applied to approaches on the same visual axis.

How it works:

As soon as the player movement or the camera movement is over, the editor awaits a few frames before cutting to the new shot. Usually, this technique works better when advancing from a full shot to a close-up, and when the player is not moving across the screen.

Let's see in which cases a cut after the movement is most helpful:

→ VERTICAL MOVEMENT
→ NEUTRAL MOVEMENT
→ CIRCULAR MOVEMENT

Editor's timeline:

VERTICAL MOVEMENT = In the following example a stationary player makes a vertical movement (taking a binder off a shelf). Once the action is completed, and the binder is in his hands, the editor cuts to the second shot where after a few moments of stillness, a new movement begins (going through the documents).

CUT AFTER THE MOVEMENT (Vertical)

The vertical movement of the arm is completed in shot 1

A new movement begins after the cut to shot 2

Editor's timeline:

NEUTRAL MOVEMENT = A stationary or moving player completes an action in the first frame (Player **'A'** turning his head towards the camera). The editor awaits a few frames then cuts to the second, wider shot, where a new movement in a neutral direction begins (**'A'** moving towards the camera).

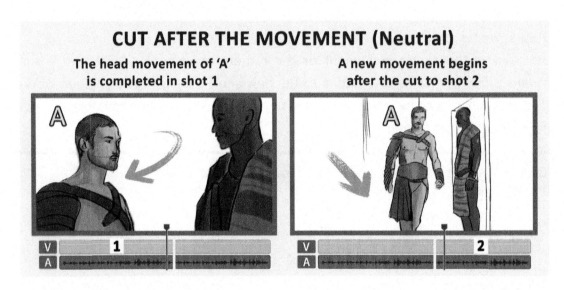

CUT AFTER THE MOVEMENT (Neutral)

The head movement of 'A' is completed in shot 1

A new movement begins after the cut to shot 2

Editor's timeline:

CIRCULAR MOVEMENT = A stationary player, **'B'**, turns his head drawing attention to another player, **'A'**, who's placed behind him, eyes shut. Once the movement is completed the editor awaits a few frames, then cuts to a closer shot of **'A'**, who eventually opens his eyes.

CUT AFTER THE MOVEMENT (Circular)

The head movement of 'B' is completed in shot 1

A new movement begins after the cut to shot 2

PART NINE

9

MATCH CUT

Editing is undoubtedly one of the most fundamental crafts of cinema (if not "the"). It would be reductive to define it as a mere set of technical skills anyone can acquire through daily repetition. This couldn't be further from the truth. The art of film editing – also known as 'montage' – potentially represents one of the rarest phenomena in the history of entertainment. There wasn't anything similar before the invention in France of the 'Cinématographe'. It took of course several decades for this new artistic expression to emerge and develop as an art form, but regardless of that, it is now – along with writing, directing, cinematography and sound – the foundation of film-making.

In a beautiful article[6] from 1956, published in the Cahiers du Cinéma, the Frenc-Swiss director Jean-Luc Godard wrote the following about film editing: *"...a brilliantly directed film gives the impression of having simply been placed end to end, but a film brilliantly edited gives the impression of having suppressed all direction"*. I couldn't agree more. It's time now to look at the craft of "cutting" through a different perspective, no more "one-third/two-thirds" principles. Let's focus now on some techniques which transform editing into a means through which creatively "move the story forward".

---

6 Montage My Fine Care, Jean-Luc Godard – Cahiers du Cinéma, December 1956.

9.1 ● Basic match cut

Definition:

Match cut = It's a basic editing technique used to preserve continuity and produce a seamless cut from one shot to another. In its most basic/common form, this type of cut *matches two shots by the action shown on screen.*

How it works:

A match cut revolves around the main idea that hiding cuts helps the flow of your edits and keeps the audience unaware of the editing process. An action starts in one frame, and after the cut, it finishes in the second frame. There might be a simple mechanical link between the shots *(cut on action)* as well as a more complex connection.

Editor's timeline:

In the following example, player **'A'** grabs his eyeglasses in shot 1 and starts to take them off. The editor cuts to shot 2 where the movement is completed (on action, therefore during the movement). This represents a very basic way of connecting two shots.

BASIC MATCH CUT

Shot 1 = The movement begins here   Shot 2 = The movement ends here

9.2 • "Visual" match cut

Definition:

"Visual" match cut = It's an editing technique used to preserve continuity and produce a seamless cut from one shot to another. A visual match cut establishes a *"visual" connection between two shots.*

How it works:

A visual match cut can exploit any subject or object present on the screen to achieve a smooth transition between two shots. It can also add meaning to an otherwise simple cut, giving the editor the opportunity to creatively jump in space and time.

It is not uncommon to use similar shapes and colours to perform a visual match cut.

Editor's timeline:

In the following example, player **'A'** grimaces in shot 1. The editor cuts to shot 2 where the same player is shown as a kid many years before, pulling the same face.

The same facial expression is used to establish a visual connection between two shots taking place in a different time and space.

VISUAL MATCH CUT

Shot 1 = First "visual" connection

Shot 2 = Second "visual" connection

9.3 • "Sonic" match cut

Definition:

"Sonic" match cut = It's an editing technique used to preserve continuity and produce a seamless cut from one shot to another. A sonic match cut establishes a "sonic" connection between two shots.

How it works:

A sonic match cut can exploit any type of sound (diegetic[7] or not, on screen or not) to achieve a smooth transition between two shots. It also works with lines of dialogue, such as when a character starts a sentence in one shot and another player finishes it in the following one. As with the visual match cut, it can help jumping in time and space throughout the narration.

Editor's timeline:

In the following example, player **'A'** screams in pain in shot 1. The editor cuts to shot 2 where an old gentleman and a young boy are screaming and applauding in a crowd of people. A similar diegetic sound is used to establish a sonic connection between two shots taking place in a different time and space.

SONIC MATCH CUT

Shot 1 = Screaming man   Shot 2 = Screaming crowd

---

7 Occurring within the context of the story and able to be heard by the characters.

PART
TEN

10

JUMP CUT

10.1 ● Jump cut

Definition:

It's *the opposite of a seamless cut.* Two shots are abruptly linked to each other, jumping from the first to the second without hiding the transition. The camera angle can change slightly, completely or stay the same.

How it works:

To perform a jump cut we just need to remove unwanted bits from a shot, or from multiple shots, regardless of how the subsequent edit will look in terms of continuity. The 30-Degree rule is one of the key rules that jump cuts often break (see chapter 10.2). Jump cuts can also be considered a variation on the ellipsis time/space technique (See chapters 11.1 and 11.2).

Before taking a look at a few examples, it's important to stress a point. The very essence of editing is in the ability of the editor to keep the flow of the film intact regardless of the cutting techniques and tricks adopted throughout the post production process. It might sound counter-intuitive to employ a tool like a jump cut – which is by its own nature an "abrupt" cut – to keep the "flow" of the edit going. But that's precisely what we've been talking about so far. If something works and serves the purpose, then go for it no matter what.

Editor's timeline:

First example = In shot 1, player **'A'** is in front of the mirror, ready to trim down his beard with a pair of scissors. Without any warning the editor cuts to shot 2, where the beard has already been trimmed and the man is now applying some foam on his face to get the remaining stubble shaved. The scene goes on through a series of similar cuts until the man is done with grooming. The whole point of the jump cut is to remove a few otherwise too long chunks of shots, which won't add anything meaningful to the main narrative. The audience is left to fill in the missing bits.

At the end of the day people know how to shave and keeping the whole sequence on screen would only achieve the goal of getting the audience bored watching something not particularly interesting nor captivating.

JUMP CUT

Shot 1 = Beginning of the scene   **Shot 2 = First of a series of jump cuts**

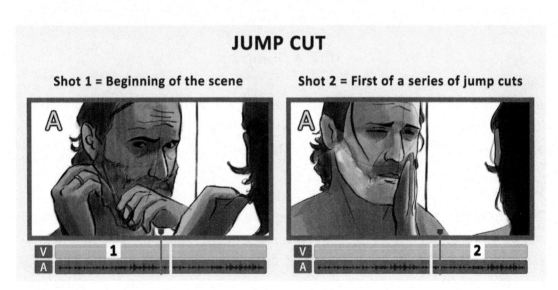

Editor's timeline:

Second example = In shot 1, player **'A'** is driving a car. Without any warning the editor cuts to shot 2, where the man is taking a gun from the glove compartment. As opposed to the previous example, the camera angle changes completely from shot 1 to shot 2.

Once again the whole point of the jump cut is to remove an otherwise too long chunk of a shot, which doesn't add anything meaningful to the main narrative. The audience is left to fill in the missing bits.

JUMP CUT

Shot 1 = Beginning of the scene

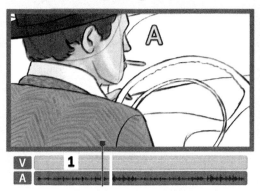

Shot 2 = First of a series of jump cuts

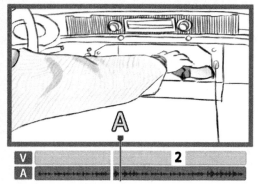

10.2 • The 30-Degree rule

Definition:

One of the key rules of *classical continuity editing*. When we cut to different shots of the same subject, it's advisable to use angles that vary by at least 30 degrees, in order to give the illusion of continuous time-space throughout the film.

THE 30-DEGREE RULE

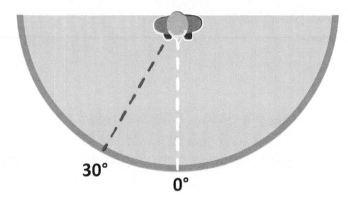

How it works:

A cut between two angles shot at less than 30 degrees from each other usually looks jarring and not pleasant to the eye. It is advisable to avoid connecting shots taken from such a close distance from each other.

THE 30-DEGREE RULE

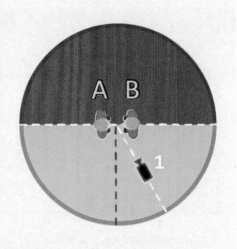

Camera position 1

THE 30-DEGREE RULE

The cut looks jarring

Camera position 2

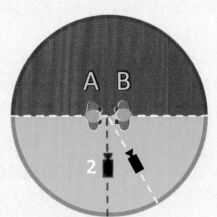

Less than 30 degrees

Editor's timeline:

In the example above there's clearly an abrupt cut on player **'A'**, from cam-1 to cam-2. The change of angle is less than 30 degrees, which results in two subsequent shots not being joined smoothly. The audience is taken aback by the "jump" and usually the narrative flow breaks. Unless there's a specific purpose or style the editor is aiming for, this rule should always be followed.

FAQ:

Q = Why should an editor use jump cuts if they break the 30-Degree rule and violate classical continuity editing?[8]

A = Continuity editing is the most popular type of editing among film-makers. That being said, It doesn't mean that there's no room for different ways of narrating a story. Besides, jump cuts are a part of the modern film language and audiences are used to them. If wisely employed, jump cuts can easily add artistic value and pace to a scene.

---

8 Editing process used to maintain consistency of time and space throughout a film.

PART
ELEVEN

11

ELLIPSIS

11.1 ● Ellipsis – space

Definition:

Type of editing technique whereby *a section* of the story related to movements within the frame (players, objects and so on) *is omitted from a scene.* It's obvious enough for the audience to fill in the missing bits.

How it works:

This powerful tool is primarily applied to an edit to improve its pace, exploit audience awareness of the basic film-making techniques and most of all to avoid boring pieces of footage to be joined together. However, sometimes *concealing parts of the shots* can be also done for narrative and dramatic purposes.

Editor's timeline:

In the following example, player **'A'** is walking within the frame from shot to shot in order to reach a destination far away from the one he set off from. The audience doesn't need to see the entirety of the soldier's walk from place to place. That would be a huge waste of *cinematic space*, adding almost nothing to the main narrative and hugely affecting the edit pace.

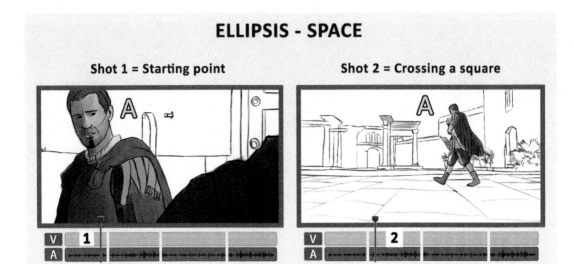

ELLIPSIS - SPACE

Shot 1 = Starting point

Shot 2 = Crossing a square

ELLIPSIS - SPACE

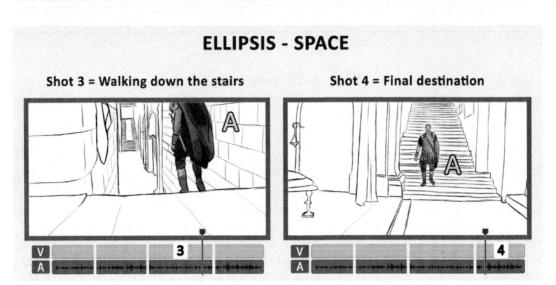

Shot 3 = Walking down the stairs

Shot 4 = Final destination

11.2 ● Ellipsis – time

Definition:

Type of editing technique whereby *a section* of the story related to the *passage of time* within the scene *is omitted from a scene.* It's obvious enough for the audience to fill in the missing bits.

How it works:

Just as for the Ellipsis – space tool, this powerful technique is primarily used to avoid the use of redundant shots and improve the overall pace. In order to achieve the *"passage of time effect"*, the editor usually cuts to a close-up or insert from the later shot, which seems to belong to the previous one (something also called *"deceptive visual cut"*). But more often the passage of time is achieved through a simple jump cut. It's advisable to exploit this tool for dramatic purposes and to speed up the pace of an otherwise too long scene.

Editor's timeline:

In the following example, we're in a parlour. **'A'** and **'B'** are standing by the door, **'C'** and **'D'**, are sitting on a sofa. In the first part of the scene, **'B'** gets introduced by **'A'** to the ladies who react to his introduction. The editor then cuts to a close-up shot of a teapot. The camera tilts up revealing **'B'** sitting in an armchair, opposite **'C'** and **'D'**.

ELLIPSIS - TIME

Shot 1 = Introducing 'B'   Shot 2 = Reaction from 'C' and 'D'

ELLIPSIS - TIME

Shot 3 (Head) = Cut to teapot.
The camera starts to tilt up

Shot 3 (Tail) = Cam movement ends.
'B' is revealed to the audience

The passage of time is brilliantly achieved because the audience has the illusion of still being in the first part of the scene when the cut to the teapot occurs (but we are actually already in part 2 and **'B'** is already sitting in the armchair).

In a nutshell:

The combination of both techniques – Ellipsis time/space – within the same scene must be considered one of the most valuable tools an editor can become familiar with. Throughout the editing process, getting rid of useless parts of shots is not only necessary, it is the very backbone of this craft.

FAQ:

Q = What's the difference between a Jump cut and an Ellipsis?

A = Both techniques share some common traits. The editor gets rid of useless footage in order to compress the filmic time and space. However, while a jump cut usually stands out on the screen as an abrupt cut, the ellipsis technique can be more subtle and complex from an editing standpoint.

PART TWELVE

12

IMPACT CUT vs THEMATIC CUT

12.1 ● Impact cut & Impact move
12.2 ● Thematic cut & Thematic move

12.1 ● Impact cut & Impact move

Definition:

Impact cut = Also known as *smash cut*, it's a type of cut from one shot to another that specifically emphasizes contrast, opposites or violence. The surprise effect can also be achieved through a camera movement *(impact move)*.

How it works:

The best way to achieve a great impact cut is by *surprising the audience with unexpected connections between shots* or scenes. Sound is also a part of the technique and should be exploited in combination with images. Pretty much the same principles applies to an impact move as well, though in that case the contrasting connections are within the same shot.

Editor's timeline:

In the following example, player **'A'** is having a relaxed conversation with a female character off screen (shot 1). All of a sudden, without any hint to it, the editor cuts to shot 2, where the same man is looking angry, screaming the hell out of himself. We switch very quickly from a calm vibe to a tense one. The low-angle chosen to take shot 2 further enhances the powerful contrast between the first and second part of the scene.

IMPACT CUT

Shot 1 = Player 'A' looks happy and relaxed   **Shot 2 = Player 'A' looks angry and upset**

 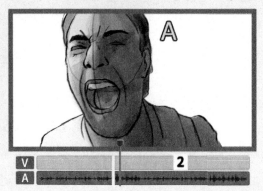

The same result can be achieved through a cam movement, as in the example below. In this case we talk about *impact move*, since the transition is achieved on set, rather than in the editing room. Yet, how the shot is used within the scene/edit/sequence, is a decision made by the editor and ultimately affects the overall movie.

IMPACT MOVE

Shot 1 (Head) = Player 'A' looks up   **Shot 1 (Tail) = Cam movement up.**
A noose is revealed to the audience

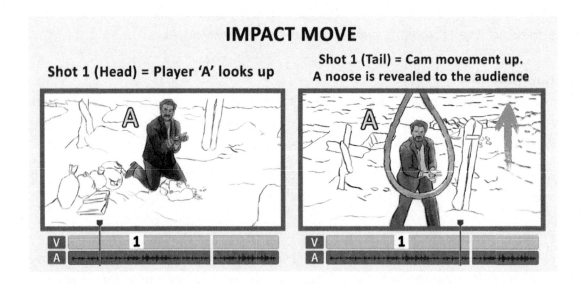

An impact move is also a great example of effective camera movement. Unfortunately after the digital technology took over in the film industry, camera movements became more and more popular and easily achievable on set. Often the vast majority of them are totally unjustifiable from a narrative point of view.

They don't really appear to move the story forward nor to serve a specific purpose, apart from achieving a frantic filming style. Shooting equipment just got much smaller and easier to carry around over the past decades. There are very few limits to the variety of shots taken by a camera operator through the use of a gimbal and a light, digital camera. Budding film-makers are often afraid of keeping the camera movements to the bare minimum – especially when it comes to dialogue scenes – as if the filmic experience could be hampered by a minimalist style of shooting (and consequently editing).

I'm a huge fan of great camera movement in chasing, fighting or action scenes in general, and I'm aware that it does enhances the viewer's feeling of engagement while watching a film. I still remember witnessing in total amazement the first flight with the mountain Banshees in Avatar (2009). I just feel at the same time that the core principles of film-making, even after evolving through times, still have a 'raison d'être', therefore finding the right balance between too much and too little might be a good idea when dealing with camera movement.

12.2 ● Thematic cut & Thematic move

Definition:

Thematic cut = It's a cut from one frame to another that emphasizes continuation of a theme, harmony or concepts connected with images that shares similar properties. Just as with the impact move, there can also be a thematic move. Let's have a look at both.

How it works:

Often film language seeks contrast. A thematic cut might therefore sound as a counter productive technique to use. However, continuity of a theme can easily be exploited as a build-up to scenes where contrast is predominant. The best way to perform a thematic cut is to make it link shots that *lead the audience logically through the story.*

Editor's timeline:

In the following example, a group of players is resting on top of a hill, overlooking the sea. The editor cuts to shot 2, which is a close up of the sea surf.

THEMATIC CUT

Shot 1 = Wide angle overlooking the sea

Shot 2 = Close up of the surf

 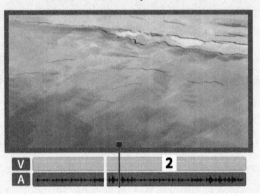

The same result can be achieved through a cam movement too, as in the example below. In this case we talk about *thematic move.* The scene opens with a close up of a bloodstained wall. The camera then pans left to reveal a dead body lying on a bed.

THEMATIC MOVE

Shot 1 (Head) = Blood stains on the wall. Cam starts to pan from right to left

Shot 1 (Tail) = Cam movement ends. A dead body is revealed to the audience

 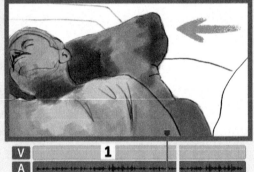

PART
THIRTEEN

13

"J" & "L" CUT

13.1 ● "J" Cut

Definition:

Type of editing technique whereby the audio from the following cut overlaps the video from the current cut and starts playing before its picture as a lead-in to it.

How it works:

Even though the J-cut is primarily used in dialogue scenes while cutting from one player to another, there's no limit to the editor's creativity when it comes to exploiting it. In a non-linear editing software[9], *this type of cut creates a shape which resembles a "J".*

Editor's timeline:

In the following example, in shot 1 we see player **'A'** holding a bunch of shrimps in his hands, while hearing his voice talking in the background, off screen. The editor cuts to shot 2, where the same man/voice can now be seen/heard on the screen.

---

9 Non-linear editing (NLE) is an editing process that enables the editor to make changes to a video or audio project without regard to the linear timeline.

'J' CUT

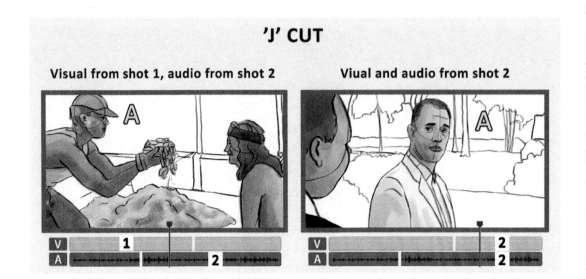

Visual from shot 1, audio from shot 2

Viual and audio from shot 2

13.2 • "L" Cut

Definition:

Type of editing technique whereby the audio from the current cut overlaps the video from the following cut and keeps playing after its picture as a lead-out from it.

How it works:

It's primarily used in dialogue scenes while cutting from one player to another. However, just as the J-cut, it's also a powerful tool to handle scene transitions. In a non-linear editing software, *this type of cut creates a shape which resembles an "L".*

Editor's timeline:

In the following example, in shot 1 we see player **'A'** holding a baby and crying her eyes out in pain. The editor cuts to shot 2, where we see the same character many years later. However the off screen/background sound, is still coming from the previous shot.

"J" and "L" cuts are far more popular than audiences are aware of. They are used constantly during scenes with dialogue, as a technique through which the editor breaks up a conversation and creates a better and more natural flow with reaction shots.

'L' CUT

Visual and audio from shot 1 **Viual from shot 2, audio from shot 1**

 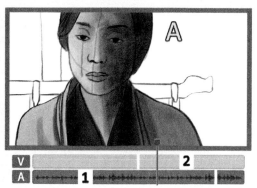

One of the most common mistakes made by inexperienced editors is to repeatedly cut on the "line of dialogue", jumping back and forth between characters in a mechanical way.

Here's a list of several movies where you can find great examples of **"J"** and **"L"** cuts. Some of them are remarkably good. I will never get tired to stress this point: film-making and editing evolved through the past Century thanks to the critical analysis of other film-makers' work. You can learn a great deal about our craft by "watching the classics" with the questions in mind of why and how someone else did what they did.

    1) *2001: A Space Odyssey (1968)*
    2) *Amadeus (1984)*
    3) *Forrest Gump (1994)*
    4) *Gladiator (2000)*
    5) *The Wolf of Wall Street (2013)*

CONCLUSIONS

You made it to the end. Thanks. Hopefully you found the content of this handbook useful enough. Perhaps you're an industry pundit who already knew most of the concepts outlined throughout the pages, in that case I hope there might still be the chance that you found that tiny piece of information that was missing in your body of knowledge. I'm aware that there were many more principles, rules and concepts I'd have loved to touch upon, such as dialogue involving a group of people, nature of movement inside the screen, players coming in and out of shot or approaching each other. The list goes on and on. I can only apologise to you for that and promise to do better next time. I've already got a hitching feeling, *Cut & Drag Vol. 2* might be on its way soon. So hang in there.

Perhaps you're instead a budding editing student, or a Guerrilla film-maker eager to learn and experiment, who's still trying to rise through the ranks. If that is the case, I'm sure that even though you might have struggled to grasp all the concepts I was trying to explain, most of them got across and hopefully resonated with you.

Here's my parting message for you: Be stubborn. Resilience is the key. No matter how high you're aiming, never give up, keep surrounding yourself with movies, books, video tutorials and any possible resource available out there which might get you where you want to be in your life. Personally I apply all the editing principles I acquired over so many years of work, to any other aspect of my life. There's method and organisation, fastidious research, but there's also emotional drive, gut feeling and pure instinct. We're humans after all, emotional creatures who connect with each other and come together to reach a common goal: bring a movie to life. Oh, and if you're wondering whether eventually I took that Degree in Law or not, the short answer is yes, I did get my Bachelor's Degree in Law, but it took me eight years rather than three. I was too busy studying editing and film-making for the remaining five.

ACKNOWLEDGEMENTS

I would like to express my special thanks to the people who helped me with this book:

Veronica Spinoni

Angela Salzano

Rachel Fowler

Alexis Currin

ILLUSTRATIONS

The author acknowledges the copyright owners of the following motion pictures from which single frames have been turned into original illustrations (by the wonderful Veronica Spinoni) and used in this book for purposes of commentary, criticism, scholarship under the Fair Use Doctrine. No endorsement or sponsorship of this book by the copyright owners is claimed or implied.

PART 1 – EDITING IS STORYTELLING
Chapter 1.1

Gladiator, © 2000 Dreamworks LLC and Universal Studios.

Chapter 1.2

Kubo and the Two Strings, © 2016 Focus Features LLC.

Chapter 1.3

The graduate, © 1967 Embassy Pictures and United Artists.

Chapter 1.4

Memories of the sword, © 2015 Lotte Entertainment.

Chapter 1.5

For a few dollars more, © 1965 PEA and United Artists.

Chapter 1.6

Pride and prejudice, © 2005 Focus Features LLC and Universal Pictures.

PART 2 – FILM EDITING TO THE RESCUE
Chapter 2.1

Catch me if you can, © 2002 Dreamworks LLC.

Chapter 2.2

Braveheart, © 1995 Paramount Pictures and 20th Century Fox.

Chapter 2.3

I, Robot, © 2004 20th Century Fox.

Chapter 2.4

One flew over the cuckoo's nest, © 1975 United Artists.

PART 4 – BASIC TOOLS

Chapter 4.1

The sea of trees, © 2015 Grand Experiment, LLC.

Chapter 4.2

The Good, the Bad and the Ugly, © 1966 Produzioni Europee Associate.

PART 5 – DIALOGUE: TWO PLAYERS/ACTORS

Chapter 5.1

Paper moon, © 1973 Paramount Pictures.

Thin ice, © 2011 ATO Pictures.

Ripper Street S3-E6, © 2012-2016 Endemol UK.

Chapter 5.2

Spartacus: Vengeance S2-E8, © 2010-2013 Starz media.

A perfect world, © 1993 Warner Bros.

The Good, the Bad and the Ugly, © 1966 Produzioni Europee Associate.

Chapter 5.3

Dark Angel S1-E1, © 2016 Endemol Shine UK.

Andrei Rublev, © 1966 Mosfilm.

A perfect world, © 1993 Warner Bros.

Chapter 5.4

Gladiator, © 2000 Dreamworks LLC and Universal Studios.

Paper moon, © 1973 Paramount Pictures.

Ripper Street S2-E8, © 2012-2016 Endemol UK.

A perfect world, © 1993 Warner Bros.

Reservoir dogs, © 1992 Miramax Films.

Chapter 5.5

Ripper Street S2-E7, © 2012-2016 Endemol UK.

Easy rider, © 1969 Columbia Pictures.

Chapter 5.6

Ripper Street S3-E4, © 2012-2016 Endemol UK.

A perfect world, © 1993 Warner Bros.

Ripper Street S2-E6, © 2012-2016 Endemol UK.

Ripper Street S2-E8, © 2012-2016 Endemol UK.

Spartacus: Blood and sand S1-E5, © 2010-2013 Starz media.

Ripper Street S2-E6, © 2012-2016 Endemol UK.

PART 6 – LINE OF INTEREST VS LINE OF ACTION

<u>Chapter 6.1</u>

The Good, the Bad and the Ugly, © 1966 Produzioni Europee Associate.

<u>Chapter 6.2</u>

Empire of the sun, © 1987 Warner Bros. Pictures.

<u>Chapter 6.3</u>

True detective S1-E1, © 2014-2019 Warner Bros. Television Distribution.

PART 7 – DIALOGUE: THREE PLAYERS/ACTORS

<u>Chapter 7.1</u>

Ripper Street S4-E1, © 2012-2016 Endemol UK.

Undrafted, © 2016 Vertical Entertainment.

<u>Chapter 7.2</u>

Forrest Gump, © 1994 Paramount Pictures.

Black Sails S1-E5, © 2016 Vertical Entertainment.

<u>Chapter 7.3</u>

Catch me if you can, © 2002 Dreamworks LLC.

Forrest Gump, © 1994 Paramount Pictures.

Vikings S4-E17, © 2013-2020 MGM Television.

<u>Chapter 7.4</u>

Ordinary person, © 2017 Opus Pictures.

Asura: The city of madness, © 2016 CJ Entertainment

Amadeus, © 1984 Orion Pictures and Thorn EMI Screen Entertainment.

Ripper Street S3-E1, © 2012-2016 Endemol UK.

Bad boys 2, © 2003 Sony Pictures Releasing.

<u>Chapter 7.5</u>

Ripper Street S3-E4, © 2012-2016 Endemol UK.

A perfect world, © 1993 Warner Bros.

Ripper Street S2-E2, © 2012-2016 Endemol UK.

Ripper Street S2-E8, © 2012-2016 Endemol UK.

PART 8 – CUT ON ACTION vs CUT AFTER THE MOVEMENT

Chapter 8.1

Harakiri, © 1962 Shochiku.

Chapter 8.2

All Good Things, © 2010 Warner Bros.

The Terminator, © 1984 Magnolia Pictures and The Weinstein Company.

Chapter 8.3

Ripper Street S3-E1, © 2012-2016 Endemol UK.

Spartacus: Blood and sand S1-E6, © 2010-2013 Starz media.

Spartacus: Blood and sand S1-E7, © 2010-2013 Starz media.

PART 9 – MATCH CUT

Chapter 9.1

Ripper Street S3-E6, © 2012-2016 Endemol UK.

Chapter 9.2

Forrest Gump, © 1994 Paramount Pictures.

Chapter 9.3

Ripper Street S2-E8, © 2012-2016 Endemol UK.

PART 10 – JUMP CUT

Chapter 10.1

The walking dead S2-E12, © 2010-2020 AMC Networks

Breathless, © 1960 Société nouvelle de cinématographie.

Chapter 10.2

Ripper Street S2-E7, © 2012-2016 Endemol UK.

PART 11 – ELLIPSIS

Chapter 11.1

Risen, © 2016 Sony Pictures Releasing.

Chapter 11.2

Ripper Street S2-E6, © 2012-2016 Endemol UK.

PART 12 – IMPACT CUT vs THEMATIC CUT

Chapter 12.1

All Good Things, © 2010 Warner Bros.

The Good, the Bad and the Ugly, © 1966 Produzioni Europee Associate.

<u>Chapter 12.2</u>

Risen, © 2016 Sony Pictures Releasing.

Ripper Street S2-E1, © 2012-2016 Endemol UK.

PART 13 – "J" CUT & "L" CUT

<u>Chapter 13.1</u>

Forrest Gump, © 1994 Paramount Pictures.

<u>Chapter 13.2</u>

Memories of the sword, © 2015 Lotte Entertainment.

ESSENTIAL BIBLIOGRAPHY

Arijon, Daniel • *Grammar of the film language.* Los Angeles: Silman-James Press (1991).

Brown, Blain • *Motion Picture and Video Lighting.* London: Routledge (2007). Los Angeles: Silman-James Press (1991).

Campbell Joseph • *The Hero with A Thousand Faces (The Collected Works of Joseph Campbell).* Novato: New world library (2008).

Crittenden Roger • *Fine Cuts. The art of European film editing.* Burlington: Focal press (2013).

Dunlop, Renee • *Production pipeline fundamentals for film and games.* Burlington: Focal press (2014).

Evans Russell • *Manuale pratico per filmakers.* Roma: Dino Audino Editore (2007).

Howard D., Mabley E. • *Gli strumenti dello sceneggiatore.* Roma: Dino Audino Editore (1999).

Hullfish, Steve • *Art of the cut. Conversations with film and Tv editors.* New York: Routledge (2017).

Indick, William • *Psychology for screenwriters. Building conflict in your script.* Los Angeles: Michael Wiese Productions (2004).

Katz, Steven D. • *Film directing, cinematic motion.* Los Angeles: Michael Wiese Productions (2004).

Kenworthy, Christopher • *Master Shots Vol 1, 2nd Edition: 100 Advanced Camera Techniques to Get an Expensive Look on Your Low-Budget Movie.* Los Angeles: Michael Wiese Productions (2012).

Lumet, Sidney • *Making movies.* London: Bloomsbury (1996).

Mascelli, Joseph V. • *L'ABC della ripresa cinematografica.* Roma: Dino Audino Editore (2005).

Murch, Walter • *In the blink of an eye. A perspective on film editing.* Los Angeles: Silman-James Press (2001).

Rabiger, Michael • *Girare un film vol I. Manuale pratico di regia: dall'idea alla sceneggiatura al casting.* Roma: Dino Audino Editore (2004).

Rabiger, Michael • *Girare un film vol II. Manuale pratico di regia: dalla recitazione alle riprese al montaggio.* Roma: Dino Audino Editore (2004).

Rodriguez, Robert • *Rebel Without a Crew: Or How a 23-Year-Old Filmmaker with $7,000 Became a Hollywood Player.* New York: Penguin group (1996).

Rondolino, Gianni • *Storia del cinema_1.* Torino: UTET libreria (2006).

Rondolino, Gianni • *Storia del cinema_2.* Torino: UTET libreria (2006).

Rowlands Avril • *Continuity in film and video.* Cambridge: Focal Press (1989).

Sonnenschein, David • *Sound design. The expressive power of music, voice, and sound effects in Cinema.* Los Angeles: Michael Wiese Productions (2001).

Trottier, David • *The screenwriter's bible.* Los Angeles: Silman-James Press (2005).

Vineyard, Jeremy • *Setting up your shots: great camera moves every filmmaker should know.* Los Angeles: Michael Wiese Productions (2008).

Vogler, Christopher • *Writer's journey.* Los Angeles: Michael Wiese Productions (2007).

SUBJECT INDEX